THE AMAZING BOOK OF
USELESS
INFORMATION

More Things You Didn't Need to Know
But Are About to Find Out

NOEL BOTHAM
AND THE USELESS INFORMATION SOCIETY

A PERIGEE BOOK

A PERIGEE BOOK
Published by the Penguin Group
Penguin Group (USA) Inc.
375 Hudson Street, New York, New York 10014, USA
Penguin Group (Canada), 90 Eglinton Avenue East, Suite 700, Toronto, Ontario M4P 2Y3, Canada
(a division of Pearson Penguin Canada Inc.)
Penguin Books Ltd., 80 Strand, London WC2R 0RL, England
Penguin Group Ireland, 25 St. Stephen's Green, Dublin 2, Ireland (a division of Penguin Books Ltd.)
Penguin Group (Australia), 250 Camberwell Road, Camberwell, Victoria 3124, Australia
(a division of Pearson Australia Group Pty. Ltd.)
Penguin Books India Pvt. Ltd., 11 Community Centre, Panchsheel Park, New Delhi—110 017, India
Penguin Group (NZ), 67 Apollo Drive, Rosedale, North Shore 0632, New Zealand
(a division of Pearson New Zealand Ltd.)
Penguin Books (South Africa) (Pty.) Ltd., 24 Sturdee Avenue, Rosebank, Johannesburg 2196,
South Africa

Penguin Books Ltd., Registered Offices: 80 Strand, London WC2R 0RL, England

While the author has made every effort to provide accurate telephone numbers and Internet addresses at
the time of publication, neither the publisher nor the author assumes any responsibility for errors, or for
changes that occur after publication. Further, the publisher does not have any control over and does not as-
sume any responsibility for author or third-party websites or their content.

Copyright © 2008 by Noel Botham
Cover design by Ben Gibson
Text design by Tiffany Estreicher

First edition: August 2008

Library of Congress Cataloging-in-Publication Data

Botham, Noel, 1940–
    The amazing book of useless information : more things you didn't need to know but are about to find
out / Noel Botham, and the Useless Information Society.— 1st ed.
        p. cm.
    "A Perigee book."
    ISBN 978-0-399-53468-3
    1. Curiosities and wonders.   2. Handbooks, vade mecums, etc.   I. Useless Information Society.
II. Title.
    AG243.B658   2008
    031.02—dc22   2008003910

PRINTED IN THE UNITED STATES OF AMERICA

10   9   8   7   6   5   4   3   2

Most Perigee books are available at special quantity discounts for bulk purchases for sales promotions,
premiums, fund-raising, or educational use. Special books, or book excerpts, can also be created to fit specific needs. For details, write: Special Markets, Penguin Group (USA) Inc., 375 Hudson Street, New York,
New York 10014.

Members of The Useless Information Society

Chairman
NOEL BOTHAM
General Secretary
KEITH WATERHOUSE
Beadle
KENNY CLAYTON
Chaplain
FATHER MICHAEL SEED
MICHAEL DILLON
BRIAN HITCHEN
ALASDAIR LONG
TIM WOODWARD
RICHARD LITTLEJOHN
STEVE WALSH
STRUAN RODGER
GAVIN HANS-HAMILTON
ASHLEY LUFF

SUGGS
MIKE MALLOY
MICHAEL BOOTH
JOHN PAYNE
BARRY PALIN
JOSEPH CONNOLLY
TONY COBB
JOHN MCENTEE
JOHN BLAKE
JOHN ROBERTS
BILL HAGGARTY
CHARLES LOWE
JOHN KING
KEN STOTT
RICHARD CORRIGAN
CONNER WALSH
JOHN TAYLOR

CONTENTS

LINGUISTICALLY CHALLENGED

ORIGIN STORIES

The study of word origins is called etymology.

The word "honcho" comes from a Japanese word meaning "squad leader" and first came into usage in the English language during the American occupation of Japan following World War II.

"Second string," meaning "replacement or backup," comes from the Middle Ages. An archer always carried a second string in case the one on his bow broke.

No term existed for "homosexuality" in ancient Greece—there were only a variety of expressions referring to specific homosexual roles. Experts find this baffling, as the old Greek culture regarded male/male love in the highest regard. According to several linguists, the word "homosexual" was not coined until 1869 by the Hungarian physician Karoly Maria Benkert.

The word "coach" is derived from the word *kocsi*, a wagon from the village of Kocs, Hungary.

"Long in the tooth," meaning "old," was originally used to describe horses. As horses age, their gums recede, giving the impression that their teeth are growing. The longer the teeth look, the older the horse.

"Aromatherapy" is a term coined by French chemist René Maurice Gattefossé in the 1920s to describe the practice of using essential oils taken from plants, flowers, roots, and seeds in healing.

The phrase "on cloud nine" originally referred to the Cumulonimbus cloud, which is the tallest of all the types of cloud genera and was originally number nine on the list developed at the 1896 International Meteorological Conference. However, the order of cloud genera was later changed and Cumulonimbus is now listed at number ten.

ALPHABETICAL ORDER

The world's largest alphabet is Cambodian, with 74 letters.

There are roughly 6,500 spoken languages in the world today. However, about 2,000 of those languages have fewer than 1,000 speakers. The most widely spoken language in the world is Mandarin Chinese, with 885 million speakers in China alone.

There is a word in the English language with only one vowel, which occurs six times: indivisibility.

"Strengths" is the longest word in the English language with just one vowel.

Anagrams amused the ancient Greeks, Romans, and Hebrews, and were popular during the Middle Ages.

LOOKING FOR MEANINGS

The "O" when used as a prefix in Irish surnames means "descendant of."

The word "set" has the highest number of separate definitions in the English language, with 192 definitions according to the *Oxford English Dictionary*.

The "ZIP" in ZIP code stands for Zoning Improvement Plan.

A magic potion or charm thought to arouse sexual love, especially toward a specific person, is known as a "philter."

The first episode of *Joanie Loves Chachi* was the highest-rated U.S. television episode in the history of Korean television. *Chachi* is Korean for "penis."

In Finnish, *pääjääjää*, meaning "the main stayer," has 14 dots in a row.

VOCATION VOCABULARY

A speleologist studies caves.

A bibliophile is a collector of rare books. A bibliopole is a seller of rare books.

Cannibalism, eating human flesh, is also called anthropophagy.

A person that irons wrinkles from shoes as they are being made to ensure that they stay smooth is called a wrinkle chaser.

A vermiculturist is also known as a worm farmer.

A chicken sexer is a person who distinguishes the sex of chicken hatchlings.

🌰 BREVITY IS THE SOUL OF WIT

The shortest complete sentence in the English language is "Go."

WHAT IS UP?

There is a two-letter word that perhaps has more meaning than any other two-letter word . . . and that is "UP." If you are not confused after reading this, you must really be messed "UP."

It's easy to understand UP, meaning toward the sky or at the top of the list, but when we waken in the morning, why do we wake UP?

At a meeting, why does a topic come UP?

Why do we speak UP, and why are the officers UP for

election, and why is it UP to the secretary to write UP a report?

We call UP our friends, we use paint to brighten UP a room, we polish UP the silver, we warm UP the leftovers, and clean UP the kitchen. We lock UP the house, and some guys fix UP the old car.

People stir UP trouble, line UP for tickets, work UP an appetite, and think UP excuses. To be dressed is one thing, but to be dressed UP is special.

A drain must be opened UP because it is stopped UP. We open UP a store in the morning, but we close it UP at night.

When it threatens to rain, we say it is clouding UP. When the sun comes out, we say it is clearing UP. When it rains, it wets UP the earth. When it doesn't rain for a while, things dry UP.

We seem to be pretty mixed UP about UP.

To be knowledgeable about the proper uses of UP, look UP the word in the dictionary. In a desk-size dictionary, UP takes UP almost a quarter of the page and definitions add UP to about thirty.

If you are UP to it, you might try building UP a list of the many ways UP is used. It will take UP a lot of your time, but, if you don't give UP, you may wind UP with a hundred or more.

HOT HOMONYMS

The bandage was wound around the wound.

The farm was used to produce produce.

The dump was so full that it had to refuse more refuse.

We must polish the Polish furniture.

He could lead if he would get the lead out.

The soldier decided to desert his dessert in the desert.

Since there is no time like the present, he thought it was time to present the present.

A bass was painted on the head of the bass drum.

When shot at, the dove dove into the bushes.

I did not object to the object.

The insurance was invalid for the invalid.

There was a row among the oarsmen about how to row.

They were too close to the door to close it.

The buck does strange things when the does are present.

A seamstress and a sewer fell down into a sewer line.

To help with planting, the farmer taught his sow to sow.

The wind was too strong for us to wind the sail.

After a number of injections, my jaw got number.

Upon seeing the tear in the painting, I shed a tear.

I had to subject the subject to a series of tests.

How can I intimate this to my most intimate friend?

APT ANAGRAMS

DORMITORY rearranged is DIRTY ROOM

PRESBYTERIAN rearranged is BEST IN PRAYER

ASTRONOMER rearranged is MOON STARER

DESPERATION rearranged is A ROPE ENDS IT

THE EYES rearranged is THEY SEE

GEORGE BUSH rearranged is HE BUGS GORE

THE MORSE CODE rearranged is HERE COME DOTS

SLOT MACHINES rearranged is CASH LOST IN 'EM

EVANGELIST rearranged is EVIL'S AGENT

ANIMOSITY rearranged is IS NO AMITY

ELECTION RESULTS rearranged is LIES—LET'S RECOUNT

SNOOZE ALARMS rearranged is ALAS! NO MORE ZS

A DECIMAL POINT rearranged is I'M A DOT IN PLACE

THE EARTHQUAKES rearranged is THAT QUEER SHAKE

ELEVEN PLUS TWO rearranged is TWELVE PLUS ONE

MOTHER-IN-LAW rearranged is WOMAN HITLER

POP QUIZ

a) How long did the Hundred Years' War last?

b) Which country makes Panama hats?

c) From which animal do we get catgut?

d) In which month do Russians celebrate the October Revolution?

e) What is a camel's hair brush made of?

f) The Canary Islands in the Pacific are named after which animal?

g) What was King George VI's first name?

h) What color is a purple finch?

i) Where are Chinese gooseberries from?

Answer Key
a) 116 years b) Ecuador c) Sheep and horses
d) November e) Squirrel fur f) Dogs (Canines)
g) Albert h) Crimson i) New Zealand

Name three consecutive days without using the words Monday, Tuesday, Wednesday, Thursday, Friday, Saturday, or Sunday.

Answer Key
Yesterday, today, and tomorrow.

Count the number of Fs in the following text:
Finished files are the result of years of scientific study combined with the experience of years.

Answer Key
There are six. The brain cannot process the word "of."

BELIEF BRIEFS

THE WORDS OF THE LORD

Scholars estimate that the 66 books of the King James version of the Bible were written by some 50 different authors. These books were chosen, after a bit of haggling, by the Catholic Council of Carthage in AD 397—more than 350 years after the time of Jesus. This collection is broken into two major sections: the Old Testament, which consists of 39 books, and the New Testament, which has 27 books. (Catholic Bibles include an additional 12 books known as the Apocrypha.) The Gospels for the New Testament were chosen from a huge selection. Many were discarded or destroyed because they did not agree with the then accepted version of Christianity. In some of these other gospels, women are portrayed in very different positions—as disciples, as apostles, as teachers—than in the Gospels of the New Testament.

Long ago, when many people were unable to read the Bible, pictures were put in stained glass windows to remind them of the stories.

Gabriel, Michael, and Lucifer are the three angels mentioned by name in the Bible.

The longest name in the Bible is Mahershalalhashbaz.

The Bible does not say there were three wise men, or magi; it only says there were three gifts. Some scholars believe there were anywhere between two and nine magi.

Seven suicides are recorded in the Bible.

The Bible devotes some 500 verses on prayer, less than 500 verses on faith, but more than 2,000 verses on money and possessions.

The Red Sea is not mentioned in the Bible.

There are 49 different foods mentioned in the Bible. Salt is mentioned more than 30 times. Almonds and pistachios are the only nuts mentioned in the Bible.

The first translation of the English Bible was initiated by John Wycliffe and completed by John Purvey in 1388.

The Four Horsemen of the Apocalypse, named in the Bible's Book of Revelation, are Conquest, Slaughter, Famine, and Death.

The four Gospels, Matthew, Mark, Luke, and John, selected for inclusion in the New Testament, are examples of books that did not carry the names of their actual authors. The present names were assigned long after these four books were written. In spite of what the Gospel authors say, biblical scholars are now almost unanimously agreed that none of the Gospel authors was either a disciple of Jesus or an eyewitness to his ministry.

Jesus was described as "king of the Jews" as a deliberate insult to the Jewish authorities on the part of Pilate, the governor of Judea.

"Hagiology" is the branch of literature dealing with the lives and legends of saints.

MARY, MARY, QUITE CONTRARY

In 1854 it was decided, on a majority vote of cardinals, that Mary had been immaculately conceived. The Immaculate Conception, never mentioned in the Bible, means that Mary, whose conception was brought about the normal way, was conceived without original sin or its stain. This means God protected her from the first instant of her existence so as to be free from the corrupt nature original sin brings. This is different from her being a virgin when she conceived Jesus.

All the teaching concerning Mary as Mother of God, Queen of Heaven, Refuge of Sinners, Gate of Heaven, Mother of Mercies, Spouse of the Holy Ghost, and so on is not mentioned in the Bible. There was a time when the pope excommunicated members of the Church for praying to the Virgin Mary. The worship of Mary, today acclaimed as an infallible dogma, was once condemned by the Church as a deadly sin.

The Assumption of Mary into heaven, which was not mentioned in the Bible, did not become Catholic dogma until being formally declared by Pope Pius XII in 1950. This states that Mary's uncorrupt body was carried straight to heaven after her death.

The Gospel of Mary (Magdalene) was discovered in 1896 by Dr. Karl Reinhardt. Due to a series of unfortunate events, a translation wasn't published until 1955, when it appeared first in German. It first appeared in English along with the texts from the Nag Hammadi Library in 1977. It is missing several pages, but enough survives to draw the conclusion that at least one sect of early Christianity held Mary Magdalene in high esteem as a visionary, apostle, and leader.

It was not until 1969 that the Roman Catholic Church quietly removed all references to Mary Magdalene as a penitent sinner and harlot and began to refer to her instead as a disciple, although this has been little publicized.

CONTROVERSIAL CLERGY

The tradition of Peter being the first bishop of Rome only surfaced in the fourth century.

The letters inscribed in the pope's miter are VICARIUS FILII DEI, which is the Latin for VICAR OF

THE SON OF GOD. In Roman numerals, the letters of this title which have assigned value add up to 666. For VICARIUS: V=5, I=1, C=100, I+1, U (or V)=5; for FILII: I=1, L=50, I=1, I=1; for DEI: D=500, I=1; totaling 666, the traditional "number of the Devil."

At least four popes are known to have had illegitimate children. At least five popes were sons of priests, including at least one, or possibly two, popes who were sons of other popes. At least six popes were excommunicated or condemned as heretics, including one pope who was excommunicated twice and two popes who excommunicated one another.

In its first 12 centuries of existence, the Church was disturbed some 25 times by rival claimants of the papacy. The resulting strife was always an occasion of scandal, sometimes of violence and bloodshed.

For 40 years in the fourteenth century, there were simultaneously up to three different infallible popes. A division occurred in the Church of Rome, and the two factions vied for superiority. One faction officially elected Pope Urban VI as the head of the Church, who was succeeded by Boniface IX in 1389 and later Pope Gregory XII. The other party elected Pope Clement VII, called historically the antipope, who was succeeded by Pope Benedictine XIII in 1394 as head of the Church. Then, in 1409, a third party of reactionaries, who now claimed to represent the true Church, elected Pope Alexander V as head of the Roman hierarchy. In June

1409, Pope Alexander V officially excommunicated the other two popes, and gradually the incident was resolved.

Pope Alexander VI was born Rodrigo de Borja y Borja in 1431 and was made a cardinal at age 25 by his uncle, Pope Callistus III, who reigned from 1455 to 1458. Once pope, Alexander VI named his own 18-year-old son a cardinal, along with the brother of a papal mistress. Known as "the most notorious pope in all of history," he often left his daughter, Lucrezia, in charge of the papacy on his frequent trips away from Rome.

Pope Innocent IV supposedly often used torture to extract confessions.

Pope John XII is remembered as possibly the most morally corrupt pontiff. He was accused by some of turning the Rome's Lateran Palace into a brothel.

In the ninth century, Pope Nicholas I decreed that a cockerel would be displayed from every church steeple as a weather vane. The cockerel was used to remind all parishioners of Peter's three denials of Christ before the cock crowed, to keep them from this sin.

In the tenth century it was ruled that a cleric who experienced a wet dream would have to sing seven prescribed penitential psalms right after the fact, and in the morning he needed to sing 30 more.

CHRISTIAN CORNUCOPIA

Cardinal John Henry Newman, one of the authorities most respected by Rome, wrote in his book *The Development of the Christian Religion*: "Temples, incense, candles, votive offerings, holy water, holidays, and seasons of devotions, processions, blessing of fields, sacerdotal vestments, priests, monks and nuns are all of pagan origin."

Early Christians used red-colored eggs to symbolize the Resurrection.

The patron saint of dentists is Saint Apollonia.

Early Catholic doctrine declared that women did not have souls. Adam gave a rib to create Eve, it was claimed, but did not give a part of his soul. This belief has never been officially changed.

Bethlehem, which is considered by Christians the birthplace of Jesus, was an early shrine of the pagan god Adonis. It was believed that this god suffered a cruel death, after which he descended into hell, rose again, and then ascended into heaven. Each year there was a great festival in commemoration of his resurrection.

CONSTANTINE CATCHES ON

One of the major turning points in the history of the Christian Church occurred in AD 313, when Emperor Constantine I announced that Christians were allowed to practice their religion in the Roman Empire. Because of this edict, Christians could now compete with pagan Romans for high government positions. However, Constantine did not make Christianity the state religion or outlaw paganism; those were the actions of the later emperor, Theodosius I. Although Constantine's mother exposed him to Christianity, he did not finally declare himself a Christian until he was over forty.

In AD 325, Constantine called a meeting of Christian bishops at Nicea to decide what a Christian was, and what Christians should believe. He changed the time of the Resurrection to coincide with the festival celebrating the death and resurrection of the pagan god Attis. This celebration was held annually from March 22 to 25. Christians adopted the actual date, March 25, as the anniversary of the passion.

Constantine was the first to decree the "day of the Sun"—Sunday—as the Roman day of rest. The worship of various solar deities was very popular at the time—in fact, Christmas falls on December 25, the feast of Dies Natalis Solis Invicti, which was the birthday of the Roman god Mithras and the biggest day of the year for the sun-worshiping pagans. As most scholars believe that Jesus was actually born in the spring, it seems likely that his birthday was moved to coincide with this popular feast day.

HOLIDAY CHEER

The National Chanukah Menorah in Washington, DC, is the world's largest and is lit every year in a televised international ceremony.

Household waste increases by 25 percent between Thanksgiving and New Year's Day. Most of this extra garbage in the United States is made up of 4 million tons of discarded wrapping paper and shopping bags.

A man who lives in North Pole, Alaska, which advertises its 99705 ZIP code as Santa's ZIP code, takes it upon himself every year to answer many of the the hundreds of thousands of letters that are sent to Santa via the town's mailbox by children around the world.

The U.S. Postal Service delivers 20 billion cards and packages each holiday season between Thanksgiving and Christmas Eve.

Accounting for time zone differences, Santa has 31 hours to deliver gifts on Christmas Eve, but that still means he would have to visit 823 homes per second.

A family in the town of Neuhausen, Germany, has the distinction of owning the world's biggest nut-cracker collection: 4,334.

The first candy cane was made in Germany in 1670 when, supposedly, a choirmaster handed bent sugar sticks out to his young choir to keep the singers quiet during Christmas services. Today almost 2 billion candy canes are manufactured each year.

Charles Dickens wrote his classic story *A Christmas Carol* between October and November of 1843, and by Christmas day he had already sold 6,000 copies.

The world's largest gingerbread man was baked on February 21, 2006, in Rochester, Minnesota, and weighed 466 pounds, 6 ounces.

TIMELINE OF TRADITIONS

Many customs of the Catholic Church did not begin until sometimes centuries after the death of Christ. These are just a few of them:

The daily mass, AD 394.

Virgin Mary first called the Mother of God, fifth century.

Prayers to the Virgin, Queen of Heaven, AD 600.

The first pope (Boniface III), AD 610.

Kissing the pope's foot, AD 709.

Temporal power of the pope declared, AD 750.

Worship of images, relics, and cross, AD 788.

Holy water blessed by a priest, AD 850.

Canonization of dead saints, AD 995.

Lent and Good Friday, AD 998.

The mass first declared to be a sacrifice of Christ, AD 1050.

Celibacy of the priesthood and nuns, AD 1079.

The rosary introduced by Peter the Hermit, AD 1090.

Selling indulgences, AD 1190.

Confession of sins to a priest, AD 1215.

Adoration of the water, AD 1220.

Interpretation of Bible forbidden to laity, AD 1229.

Tradition established as infallible authority, AD 1545.

Apocryphal books added to the Bible, AD 1546.

Superstitions of the Ave Maria, AD 1588.

Immaculate Conception of the Virgin Mary, AD 1854.

Infallibility of the pope officially declared, AD 1870.

Mary officially declared to be the Mother of God, AD 1931.

SPIRITUAL STEPPING-STONES

In 1129, King Henry I began charging a tax to ecclesiastics who abandoned celibacy.

> The Hindu holy day begins at sunrise, the Jewish holy day begins at sunset, and the Christian holy day begins at midnight.

On April 6, 1830, in a small log cabin, six men including Joseph Smith and his brother Hyrum founded and publicly signed the charter for the Church of Jesus Christ of Latter-day Saints. In 1844, Joseph and his brother Hyrum were killed by an angry mob while incarcerated at Carthage Jail in Quincy, Illinois. The Mormons, now led by Brigham Young, were forced to flee the confines of the United States to the Salt Lake Valley, which at the time was part of Mexico.

> The Church of Scientology was founded in 1953, in Washington, DC, by science fiction writer L. Ron Hubbard.

FROM THEIR LIPS TO GOD'S EARS

Sensible men are all of the same religion.
Earl of Shaftesbury

To become a popular religion, it is only necessary for a superstition to enslave a philosophy.
William Ralph Inge

Prisons are built with stones of law, brothels with blocks of religion.

William Blake

There is only one religion, though there are a hundred versions of it.

George Bernard Shaw

It is a mistake to suppose that God is only, or even chiefly, concerned with religion.

William Temple

Every dictator uses religion as a prop to keep himself in power.

Benazir Bhutto

Superstition is the religion of feeble minds.

Edmund Burke

We have just enough religion to make us hate, but not enough to make us love one another.

Jonathan Swift

In matters of religion and matrimony, I never give any advice, because I will not have anybody's torments in this world or the next laid to my charge.

Lord Chesterfield

Science without religion is lame, religion without science is blind.

Albert Einstein

Religion is the sigh of the oppressed creature, the heart of a heartless world . . . It is the opium of the people.
    Karl Marx

Our religion is made so as to wipe out vices; it covers them up, nourishes them, incites them.
    Michel de Montaigne

Thanks to God, I am still an atheist.
    Luis Buñuel

Sensible men never tell.
    Earl of Shaftesbury

Things have come to a pretty pass when religion is allowed to invade the sphere of private life.
    William Lamb

An atheist is a man who has no invisible means of support.
    John Buchan

A Protestant, if he wants aid or advice on any matter, can only go to his solicitor.
    Benjamin Disraeli

The two dangers which beset the Church of England are good music and bad preaching.
    Lord Hugh Cecil

I am always most religious on a sunshiny day.
    Lord Byron

A lady, if undressed at church, looks silly; one cannot be devout in dishabille.

George Farquhar

What after all is a halo? It's only one more thing to keep clean.

Christopher Fry

Pray, good people, be civil. I am a Protestant whore.

Nell Gwyn

The spirituality of man is most apparent when he is eating a hearty dinner.

W. Somerset Maugham

Puritanism. The haunting fear that someone, somewhere, may be happy.

H. L. Mencken

People may say what they like about the decay of Christianity; the religious system that produced green Chartreuse can never really die.

Saki

God is a man, so it must be all rot.

Nancy Nicholson

Baptists are only funny under water.

Neil Simon

There's no reason to bring religion into it. I think we ought to have as great a regard for religion as we can, so as to keep it out of as many things as possible.

    Sean O'Casey

Protestant women must keep taking the Pill; Roman Catholic women must keep taking the *Tablet* [largest-circulation international Catholic newspaper].

    Eileen Thomas

Jesus is coming! Look busy!

    Bumper Sticker

Pray, what is that?

    Earl of Shaftesbury

Arithmetic Exam

A lump of cheese can be chopped into a maximum of 93 pieces with eight straight cuts.

The number four is the only number in the English language that is spelled with the same number of letters as the number itself.

Forty is the only number with all its letters in alphabetical order, and one is the only number to have its letters in reverse alphabetical order.

Twenty-nine is the only number that is written with as many strokes as its numerical value (if *Y* is written with three strokes).

An "octillion" is the lowest positive number to contain a letter *C*.

The number 172 can be found on the back of the five-dollar bill in the bushes at the base of the Lincoln Memorial.

A mile on land is 5,280 feet. A nautical mile is 6,080 feet.

A carat, the measurement of gems, is 200 milligrams, nearly the equivalent the weight of the carab seed on which it was based.

A pound of gold actually weighs less than a pound of feathers. The reason is that feathers are measured in avoirdupois weight in which there are 16 ounces per pound. Gold is measured in troy weight with 12 ounces per pound.

If 1089 is multiplied by 9, the result is the number's reverse, 9801. This also works with 10989 or 109989 or 1099989 and so on.

1 is the only positive whole number that can be added to 1,000,000 and will result in an answer that's bigger than if it is multiplied by 1,000,000.

$19 = 1 \times 9 + 1 + 9$ and $29 = 2 \times 9 + 2 + 9$. This also works for 39, 49, 59, 69, 79, 89, and 99.

153, 370, 371, and 407 are all the "sum of the cubes of their digits." In other words, $15^3 = 1^3 + 5^3 + 3^3$.

Any square number divided by 8 results in a remainder of 0, 1, or 4.

2 is the only number that gives the same result added to itself as it does multiplied by itself.

There are 12,988,816 different ways to cover a chessboard with 32 dominoes.

69 squared $= 69^2 = 4761$, and 69 cubed $= 69^3 = 328509$. These two answers use all the digits from 0 to 9 between them. As does $18^3 = 5832$, and $18^4 = 104976$.

1 divided by 37 equals 0.027027027 . . . and 1 divided by 27 equals 0.037037037.

$13^2 = 169$, and if both numbers are written backward the result is $31^2 = 961$. This also works with 12 because $12^2 = 144$, and $21^2 = 441$.

8 is the only cube that is 1 less than a square.

To multiply 10,112,359,550,561,797,752,808,988,764, 044,943,820,224,719 by 9, move the 9 at the very end up to the front. This is the only equation that can be solved in such a way.

$1 \times 9 + 2 = 11$, $12 \times 9 + 3 = 111$, $123 \times 9 + 4 = 1111$, and so on.

There are 169,518,829,100,544,000,000,000,000,000 ways to play the first ten moves in a game of chess.

3,608,528,850,368,400,786,036,725 contains 25 digits and divides evenly by 25.

The biggest number that can be made with three digits

and any operators is 9 to the power of 9 to the power of 9. As $9^9 = 387,420,489$, the final number is $9,387,420,489 =$ about 200 million digits.

> To add all the numbers from 1 to 10, divide the 10 by 2, then write the answer out twice—it equals 55. This also works when adding the numbers from 1 to 100, 1 to 1,000, and so on.

144 is the 12th number in the Fibonacci series 144 and is also the result of 12^2.

> 1,274,953,680 uses all the digits from 0 to 9 and can be divided exactly by any number from 1 to 16.

There is something curious in the properties of the number 9. Any number multiplied by 9 produces a sum of figures that, added together, continually makes 9. For example, all the first multiples of 9—18, 27, 36, 45, 54, 63, 72, 81—add up to 9. Each of them multiplied by any number produces a similar result: $8 \times 81 = 648$; these added together make 18: 1 and $8 = 9$; multiply 648 by itself, the product is 419,904—the sum of these digits is 27: $2 + 7 = 9$.

> What 5-digit number, when multiplied by the number 4, is the same number with the digits in reverse order? 21978; $21978 \times 4 = 87912$.

$111,111,111 \times 111,111,111 = 12,345,678,987,654,321$

FIRST IN LINE

LADIES FIRST!

The first First Lady was Martha Washington.

The first published American woman writer was Anne Bradstreet with *The Tenth Muse Lately Sprung Up in America* in 1650.

The first female newspaper editor was Ann Franklin, in 1762, of the *Newport Mercury* in Newport, Rhode Island.

The first American woman ordained a minister by a recognized denomination was Antoinette Brown Blackwell in 1853.

The first woman to successfully climb the Matterhorn in Switzerland was Lucy Walker in 1871.

The first woman to run for president was Victoria Woodhall in 1872.

The first immigrant to pass through Ellis Island was

Annie Moore in 1892. She was 15 years old and from County Cork, Ireland.

The first woman to appear on a U.S. postage stamp was Queen Isabella of Spain in 1893.

The first woman to go over Niagara Falls in a barrel was Annie Taylor in 1901. She was 64 years old at the time.

The first woman in the British Empire to run for a national office was Vida Goldstein in 1902. She ran for the Australian Senate when women there obtained the right to vote in all federal elections.

The first woman to swim across the English Channel in each direction was Florence Chadwick in 1951.

The first American woman to win the ladies singles tennis championship at Wimbledon was May Sutton Brandy in 1904.

The first licensed female pilot was Baroness Raymonde de la Roche of France, who learned to fly in 1909, and received ticket No. 36 on March 8, 1910.

The first reigning queen of England was Queen Mary I in 1553.

The first policewoman in the United States was Alice Wells in 1910. She was hired by the Los Angeles Police Department and was allowed to design her own uniform.

The first female combat pilot to bomb an enemy target was Lt. Kendra Williams of the U.S. Navy, who bombed enemy targets over Iraq during Operation Desert Fox in 1998.

The first female film director to have a film take in more than $100 million at the box office was Penny Marshall, with *Big*, in 1988.

The first lesbian kiss on television was the *L.A. Law* kiss between Amanda Donohoe and Michelle Green in 1991.

The first black woman in space was Mae Carol Jemison on the *Endeavor* in 1992.

The first known female serial killer in America was Aileen Wuornos. In 1992 she was charged with killing five middle-age men she met on highways while hitchhiking. She was later executed.

The first Miss America was 16-year-old Margaret Gorman, in 1921.

The first female chief of a major American Indian tribe was Wilma Mankiller, who was elected principal chief of the Cherokee nation in 1985.

The first female artist inducted into the Rock and Roll Hall of Fame was Aretha Franklin in 1987.

The first female prime minister of Britain was Margaret Thatcher in 1979.

The first child born to American colonists, on what is now Roanoke Island, North Carolina, was Virginia Dare in 1587.

The first winner of the Miss World beauty pageant, at the age of 17, was Alice Hyde in 1911.

The first footprints at Grauman's Chinese Theater (now Mann's Chinese Theater) were made by Norma Talmadge in 1927.

The first Oscar winner for Best Actress was Janet Gaynor in 1928.

The first female commercial airline pilot in the United States was Emily Warner on Frontier Airlines in 1973.

The first airline hostess was Ellen Church in 1930. She served passengers flying between San Francisco, California, and Cheyenne, Wyoming, on United Airlines.

The first transatlantic solo flight by a woman was by Amelia Earhart in 1932, who traveled from Harbor Grace, Newfoundland, to Ireland in approximately 15 hours.

The first woman to pilot the Concorde was Barbara Harmer on March 25, 1993.

The first American black female pilot was Bessie Coleman in 1921.

The first around-the-world solo flight by a woman was by Jerrie Mock in 1964.

The first woman to fly faster than the speed of sound was Jacqueline Cochrane in 1953. She piloted an F-86 Sabrejet over California at an average speed of 652.337 miles per hour.

The first woman to win an Olympic Gold Medal was Charlotte Cooper in tennis in 1900.

The first canonized American saint was Mother Frances Xavier Cabrini in 1946.

The first professional woman bullfighter was Patricia McCormick, who fought two bulls in Ciudad Juárez, Mexico, in 1952.

The first monarch to have a televised coronation was Queen Elizabeth II in 1953.

The first monarch to live in Buckingham Palace was Queen Victoria in 1837.

The first exposed breasts on television were those of film star Jayne Mansfield, who exhaled at the 1957 Academy Awards and accidentally let it all hang out.

The first woman in space was Russian cosmonaut Valentina Vladimirovna Tereshkova in 1963.

The first woman to be elected a head of state was Sirimavo Bandaraneike in 1960, who became president of Sri Lanka.

The first Jewish female prime minister and first female prime minister of Israel was Golda Meir in 1964.

The first nude centerfold was Amber Dean Smith who, in 1965, at the age of 19, was crowned "Pet of the Year" by *Penthouse* magazine.

The first woman to qualify and race at the Indianapolis 500 was Janet Guthrie in 1977.

The first test-tube baby was Louise Brown from Lancashire in 1978.

The first woman to reach the summit of Mount Everest was Junko Tabei in 1975.

The first woman to set foot on the North Pole was Fran Phillips on April 5, 1971.

🌰 LADY SECOND

The first sex-change operation was performed on George (Christine) Jorgenson in 1952.

FIRST IS THE WORST

The first criminal to be executed in the electric chair was William Kemmler in 1890 in Auburn Prison, Auburn, New York.

The first airplane fatality was Thomas Selfridge, a lieutenant in the U.S. Army Signal Corps, who was in a group evaluating the Wright plane at Fort Myers, in 1908. He was up seventy-five feet with Orville Wright when the propeller hit a bracing wire and broke, throwing the plane out of control. Selfridge was killed and Wright seriously injured.

The first president to die in office was William Harrison in 1841. At 32 days, his was also the shortest term in office.

The first indicted bank robber in the United States was Edward Smith in 1831, who was sentenced to five years' hard labor on the rock pile at Sing Sing Prison.

The first woman to be placed on the FBI's Most Wanted List, for kidnapping, extortion, and other crimes, was Ruth Eisemann-Schier in 1968.

The first train robbery in the United States was committed on October 6, 1866, by the Reno brothers, who boarded an eastbound train in Indiana wearing masks and toting guns. After clearing one safe, they tossed another out the window and jumped off the train before making an easy getaway.

In 1846, Albert Tirrell became the first person to successfully use sleepwalking as a defense for murder and arson in the United States.

READY FOR TAKEOFF

The first humans to fly were Marquis d'Arlandes and Pilatre de Rozier, who were airborne in a hot-air balloon for 20 minutes in Paris on November 21, 1783.

The first successful heavier-than-air machine flight was on December 17, 1903, at Kitty Hawk, North Carolina, when Orville Wright crawled to his prone position between the wings of the biplane he and his brother Wilbur had built. The 12-horsepower aircraft covered 120 feet in 12 seconds. Later that day, in one of four flights, Wilbur stayed up 59 seconds and covered 852 feet.

The first around-the-world commercial flight was made by Pan American airlines in January 1942.

The first person to break the sound barrier by flying faster than the speed of sound was Chuck Yeager, who flew a Bell X-1 rocket at 670 miles per hour in level flight on October 14, 1947.

The first aerial combat was in August 1914, when Allied and German pilots and observers started shooting at each other with pistols and rifles—with negligible results.

The first balloonist to fly solo around the world was Steve Fossett, who landed in Australia on July 4, 2002.

The first man to fly solo across the Atlantic was Charles Lindbergh in 1927.

INITIAL DESCENT

The first parachute jump, in 1797, was made by André-Jacques Garnerin, who was dropped from about 3,200 feet over a Paris park, in a 23-foot-diameter parachute made of white canvas with a basket attached.

The first known person to survive the jump off Niagara Falls was Sam Patch in 1829.

WE HAVE IGNITION

The first land speed record in car racing was set in 1903 by Alexander Winton, at Daytona Beach. His speed was 68.18 miles per hour.

The first winner of the Grand Prix held at Le Mans, France, was Romanian driver Ferenc Szisz in 1906, who drove a Renault.

The first person to break the sound barrier in a car, at Lake Bonneville, Utah, was Craig Breedlove, with a speed of over 760 miles an hour, in 1998.

CURTAIN UP!

The first actor to star in a talking motion picture was Al Jolson in 1927 in *The Jazz Singer*.

The first television service, airing three hours a day, was started by the BBC in 1936.

The first issue of *TV Guide* in April 1953 had Lucille Ball and her son Desi Arnaz Jr. on the cover.

The first time the word "hell" was used on television was in 1967 on *Star Trek*, when Captain Kirk said, "Let's get the hell out of here."

The first time the word "bastard" was used on television was when Meg called her son Ben a "bastard" on the soap opera *Love of Life* in 1974.

The first rape scene on television was in the controversial TV movie *Born Innocent*, starring Linda Blair, on NBC on September 10, 1974.

The first actor to portray an openly gay main character in a TV show was Billy Crystal, who played Jodie Dallas on ABC's *Soap*, which aired from 1977 to 1981.

🌰 TURN THE RADIO UP

The big band that started the swing era on radio was Benny Goodman's, on NBC's *Let's Dance* in 1934.

The first gold record ever awarded to a recording artist was to Glenn Miller in 1941.

TOP OF THE LEADERBOARD

The first winner of the Tour de France was Maurice Garin in 1903.

The first person to cross the Antarctic Circle was James Cook in 1773.

The first man to reach the South Pole, beating an expedition led by Robert F. Scott, was Norwegian explorer Roald Amundsen in 1911.

The first person to cross Niagara Falls on a tightrope was Jean François "Blondin" Gravelet in 1859.

The first flying trapeze circus act in the world, performed at the Cirque Napoleon in Paris, without safety nets, was by Jules Leotard in 1859.

The first recognized boxing champion was Tim Hyer in 1841.

The first known person to swim across the English Channel was Matthew Webb in 1875. (He drowned in 1883 after unsuccessfully trying to swim across the whirlpools and rapids beneath Niagara Falls.)

The first world chess champion was Wilhelm Steinitz in 1886.

The first winner of the U.S. Masters Golf Tournament, at Augusta National in Georgia, was Horton Smith in 1934.

The first recorded climb of Mount Everest was by Sir Edmund Hillary in 1953.

The first recorded person to run a mile race in under four minutes was Sir Roger Bannister on May 6, 1954. He broke the four-minute barrier at Imey Road, Oxford, in a time of 3 minutes 59.4 seconds.

The first figure skater to land a quadruple jump in competition was Kurt Browning in 1988.

The first athlete in a team sport to come out during his athletic career was British soccer player Justin Fashanu in 1988.

The first athlete to win seven Olympic gold medals was American swimmer Mark Spitz in 1972.

FIRST PLACE IN SPACE

The first living creature to orbit Earth was Laika the dog in 1957 aboard the Soviet satellite *Sputnik 2*.

The first human in space, and the first to orbit Earth, was Yuri Alekseyevich Gagarin in 1961.

The first black man in space was Guion Stewart Bluford Jr. in 1983.

The first human to walk in space was Alexei Arkhovich Leonov in 1965.

LEADING LEADERS

The first and the only unanimously elected U.S. president was George Washington in 1789.

The first tsar of Russia was Ivan IV (known as Ivan the Terrible) in 1547.

The first prime minister of Australia was Edmund Barton, in 1900.

The first and only U.S. president to resign from office was Richard Milhaus Nixon in 1974.

The first Pole to become pope was John Paul II, Karol Wojtyla, in 1978.

PRELIMINARY DIAGNOSES

The first person to have his diabetes successfully treated was a 14-year-old Canadian boy named Leonard Thompson, who was injected with the new discovery called insulin, at Toronto General Hospital in 1922.

The first quintuplets to survive infancy were Marie, Cecile, Yvonne, Emilie, and Annette Dionne, who were born near Callender, Ontario, to Oliva and Elzire Dionne in 1934.

The first cloned mammal was Dolly the lamb, in 1996.

The first human heart transplant was performed in 1967 by South African heart surgeon Christiaan Barnard.

The first recipient of a permanent patented artificial heart was Barney Clark on December 2, 1982. He lived until March 23, 1983.

INAUGURAL INSTANCES

The first sheets of toilet paper, each measuring two by three feet, and for use by the emperor, were introduced in China in 1391. The first toilet paper rolls were marketed by the Scott Paper Company in Philadelphia in 1879.

The first magician to perform the trick of sawing a woman in half was Count de Grisley, in 1799.

The first grapefruit trees in Florida, around Tampa Bay, were planted by Frenchman Count Odette Phillipe in 1823. Today, Florida produces more grapefruit than the rest of the world combined.

The first rubber band was made and patented in 1845.

The first skyscraper, the 10-story Wainwright Building in St. Louis, was designed by Louis Henry Sullivan in 1891.

The first bottled Coca-Cola appeared in 1899 in Chattanooga, Tennessee.

The first Scrabble game was played in 1931.

The first telephone call made around the world was in 1935.

The first male to appear on the cover of *Playboy* magazine was Peter Sellers in 1964.

The first artist on the cover of *Rolling Stone* magazine was John Lennon on November 9, 1967.

The first *People* magazine cover was of Mia Farrow in 1974.

The first item ever sold on eBay was a broken laser printer, sold for $14 by the site's creator.

The world's first active MySpace account belongs to a user named "ducky," who has almost 200,000 friends.

The world's first perfect Pac-Man game was played on July 3, 1999, by Billy Mitchell. It took him six hours to score the maximum possible 3,333,360 points by eating every fruit, Power Pellet, blue ghost, and dot for 256 boards without losing a single life. Interestingly, although the game technically has no end, the 256th and final level contains a bug that has thus far made the level impossible to finish.

The first condensed soup was made in New Jersey in 1897.

The first vending machines in the United States dispensed chewing gum and were installed in New York City train platforms in 1888.

ROMANTIC NOTIONS

XOXO

A team of medical experts in Virginia contends you're more likely to catch the common cold virus by shaking hands than by kissing.

Romantic Canadian porcupines kiss one another on the lips.

Matrimonial pollsters contend that a man who kisses his wife good-bye when he leaves for work every morning averages a higher income than a man who doesn't. Husbands who exercise the rituals of affection tend to be more painstaking, more stable, more methodical, and, thus, higher earners, it's believed. It has also been documented that men who kiss their wives before leaving home in the morning live five years longer than those who do not.

In medieval Italy, kisses weren't taken—or given—lightly; if a man and a woman were seen embracing in public, they could be forced to marry.

The longest kiss listed in the *Guinness Book of World Records* lasted an incredible 417 hours.

The German language contains 30 words that refer to the act of kissing. There is even a word, *Nachkuss*, for all the kisses that haven't yet been named.

The average woman uses up approximately her height in lipstick every five years.

SEXUAL REFERENCES

In ancient Babylon, all women were required to serve as prostitutes in the temple before getting married. Some unattractive women sometimes had to serve three or four years before finally being chosen.

On the island of Trobriand, a lover customarily bites off his lady friend's eyelashes. But he would never take her out to dinner, unless they were married. To share a meal with her would disgrace her.

In Cali, Colombia, the first time a woman has sex with her husband, her mother must also be present.

Empress Hu of the Northern Qi dynasty engaged in

"immoral play" with her eunuchs and had an affair with one of her husband's officials. As empress dowager, she had an affair with a Buddhist monk and opened a brothel with her daughter-in-law, reportedly remarking, "Being a prostitute is more pleasurable than being an empress."

Until recently, among some tribes in New Guinea it was the custom for a young fighting man to give his girlfriend a finger cut from the hand of his opponent. She wore the finger on a string around her neck. Some elderly natives there still have missing fingers.

Recent research indicates that about 9,000 romantic couples take out marriage licenses each year, then fail to use them.

In 1869, Dr. George Taylor invented the world's first vibrator, called the manipulator. It was powered by steam and was intended as a cure for just about any medical problem a woman had.

The least expensive prostitutes in the world are the Petrapole people, who live on the border of Bangladesh. They charge as little as 10 rupees, which is the equivalent of 92 cents.

There are 2.5 million new gonorrhea cases a year among Americans.

✒ UNLAWFUL BEHAVIOR

The United States has more laws governing sexual behavior than every country in Europe combined.

An excerpt from Kentucky state legislation: "No female shall appear in a bathing suit on any highway within this state unless she be escorted by at least two officers or unless she be armed with a club."

In Oxford, Ohio, it's illegal for a woman to strip off her clothes in front of a man's picture.

In Maryland, it is illegal to sell condoms from vending machines, with one exception—prophylactics may be dispensed from a vending machine only "in places where alcoholic beverages are sold for consumption on the premises."

In Mississippi, S&M is against the law, specifically: "The depiction or description of flagellation or torture by or upon a person who is nude or in undergarments or in a bizarre or revealing costume for the purpose of sexual gratification."

In North Carolina, it is illegal to have sex with a drunken fish.

In the state of Utah, sex with an animal—unless performed for profit—is not considered sodomy and therefore is legal.

GENDER BENDERS

Women can talk longer with less effort than men, as the vocal cords of women are shorter than those of men and so release less air through them to carry the sound.

The perception that women talk three times as much as men is false. Both genders speak about sixteen thousand words a day. However, the topics of conversation do differ; researchers report that men talk about technology, sports, and money, while women talk about relationships.

Men can read smaller print than women.

Studies by Dr. Karl F. Robinson of Northwestern University reportedly prove that men change their minds two or three times more often than women.

Among transsexuals who choose sex-change operations, females who elect to become males are reportedly happier and better adjusted after the procedures than males who elect to become female.

LIKE A VIRGIN

There are more 20-year-old virgins now than there were in the late 1950s.

In ancient Greece, young aristocratic women were deflowered by having their hymens pierced by a stone penis before marrying.

In the Aztec culture, avocados were considered so sexually powerful that virgins were restricted from having contact with them.

A parthenologist is someone who specializes in the study of virgins and virginity.

O, BABY!

Both women and men are most likely to have their first orgasm alone.

According to *Playboy*, black women are 50 percent more likely than white women to have an orgasm when they have sex.

The most female orgasms per hour on record is a staggering 134. The most male orgasms per hour is just 16.

Marilyn Monroe, the most celebrated sex icon of the twentieth century, confessed to a friend that, despite her three husbands and a parade of lovers, she had never had an orgasm.

DARING DUDS

Beau Brummell started the craze for ultratight men's trousers in the early nineteenth century. Because they were so tight, the penis needed to be held to one side so as not to create an unsightly bulge. To accomplish this, some men had their penis pierced to allow it to be held by a hook on the inside of the trousers; this piercing was called a "dressing ring" because tailors would ask if a gentleman "dressed" to the left or the right and tailor the trousers accordingly. Tailors to this day will ask men if they dress to the left or right.

Approximately 3 million women in the United States sport tattoos. More than 8 million women in the country have some form of permanent makeup.

The first nipple rings, called bosom rings, appeared in Victorian Europe in the 1890s. They became fashionable among women, who often wore them joined together by a small gold chain.

According to a market research firm, the most popular American bra size is currently 36C, up from 1991 when it was 34B.

The earliest breast implants were done in the 1940s by Japanese prostitutes hoping to entice American GIs. They injected their breasts with liquid silicon.

X-PERT INTERESTS

The most successful X-rated movie of all time is *Deep Throat*. It cost less than $50,000 to make and has earned more than $100 million to date.

Porn star Annie Sprinkle claims to have had sex with 3,000 men.

For every "normal" web page, there are five porn pages.

A GAY OLD TIME

According to a 1996 study, homophobic men show a higher arousal rate when shown gay porn than men with ambivalent attitudes toward homosexuals do.

Male bats have the highest rate of homosexuality of any mammal.

Flamingos and other birds display homosexual behavior, sometimes forming committed same-sex relationships that can involve sex, traveling, living together, and raising young together.

J. Edgar Hoover, Oscar Wilde, Chief Crazy Horse, Pope Paul II, Pope Julius III, Leonard Bernstein, Alexander the Great, Sigmund Freud, Lawrence of Arabia, Plato, Peter Tchaikovsky, and Florence Nightingale were all rumored to be gay or bisexual.

PENILE SYSTEM

The average male member in all its glory is six inches long and five inches in circumference. The smallest erect penis on record was one centimeter long.

The male fetus is capable of attaining an erection during the last trimester.

A man's penis not only shrinks during cold weather but

also from nonsexual excitement such as when his favorite football team scores a touchdown.

Semen contains small amounts of more than 30 elements, including fructose, ascorbic acid, cholesterol, creatine, citric acid, lactic acid, nitrogen, vitamin B_{12}, and various salts and enzymes.

Impotence is grounds for divorce in 24 U.S. states.

The left testicle usually hangs lower than the right for right-handed men. The opposite is true for lefties.

The first sperm banks opened in 1964, in Tokyo and Iowa City.

Swans are the only birds with penises.

WOMANLY FIGURES

Women who went to college are more likely to enjoy both the giving and receiving of oral sex than high school dropouts are.

According to statistics, Australian women are most likely to have sex on the first date.

Women are most likely to want to have sex when they are ovulating.

The female bedbug has no sexual opening. To get around this dilemma, the male uses his curved penis to drill a vagina into the female.

Seventy percent of women would rather have chocolate than sex, according to a poll taken in a 1995 popular women's magazine.

TITILLATING TRADITIONS

A "buckle bunny" is a woman who goes to rodeos with the express intent of having sex with a rodeo cowboy.

Oculolinctus is a fetish whereby people are sexually aroused by licking a partner's eyeball.

Exhibitionists are most likely to be married men.

Around the world, people are having sex an average of 103 times a year. In terms of consistency, the French get it on an average of 137 times a year. The Greeks come a close second at 133 times, and the Hungarians third at 131 times per year. The United States manages an average of only 111 times a year. In Hong Kong and Singapore, they manage only 79 times, and Japan comes in last, managing just 46 times a year.

According to CNN, a study performed by Anthony Bogaert, a psychologist and human sexuality expert in Ontario, revealed that about 1 in 100 people are completely asexual, having no interest in sex at all.

A medical study conducted in Pennsylvania showed that people who have sex once or twice a week slightly boost their immune systems.

Twenty-five percent of sexually active people engage in anal sex.

Jews and atheists tend to have more sexual partners than Catholics or Protestants.

WHEN IN ROME

QUALITY OF LIFE REPORT

The ancient city of Rome at one time boasted 2 million residents.

> The forum was the main focal point and meeting place of a Roman city and the site of religious and civic buildings.

Roman law stated that prostitutes were to either dye their hair blond or wear a blond wig to separate themselves from the respectable brunette female citizens of Rome.

> Wealthy Romans, both men and women, would have all their body hair plucked, including pubic hair.

Unwanted Roman babies were usually left on rubbish heaps to die.

> It was an offense to obstruct the flow of water, punishable by a fine of 10,000 sesterces.

Rome's Circus Maximus was the biggest stadium, with seating for 250,000, and was mainly used for chariot racing.

The Romans wrote a set of laws that became the basis for many of the legal systems of Europe and Latin America. They were the first to create sculptures that actually resembled people they were supposed to portray. They also developed Roman numerals, which are still used today.

The Romans enjoyed a variety of ball games, including handball, *expulsim ludere*, soccer, and field hockey. They also played a wide variety of board games, including dice (*tesserae*), Roman chess (*latrunculi*), merels, *duodecim scripta*, tic-tac-toe (*terni lapilli*), Roman backgammon (*tabula*), and others.

Capital punishment was often carried out in the amphitheater as part of the morning entertainment, requiring condemned criminals to either face wild animals without the benefit of weapons and armor or, unprotected by any kind of armor, fight each other with swords to the death.

While "roman" is actually the root word for "romance," there wasn't a lot of it in ancient Rome when it came to marriage. Roman girls were not allowed to fall in love and choose their own husbands—marriages were arranged for them by their families. There was no religious ceremony, and no legal record made of the marriage apart from an oral contract. A marriage was recognized when a man and woman agreed to live together, or when there was evidence of a dowry having been paid.

In the second century, Romans produced glass vessels at a rate that would not be seen again in the civilized world for more than a thousand years.

In ancient Rome, there were two ways of telling time: the sundial or the water clock. The day had 12 hours and the night had 12 hours. Noon was always the sixth hour of the day, and midnight the sixth hour of the night, no matter what the season, or the fact that the length of hours changed according to the time of year.

In ancient Rome, it was considered a sign of leadership to be born with a crooked nose.

Roman boys were educated and expected to be able to read, write, and count, and, most important, to be effective speakers. Other important subjects taught to boys were law, history, Roman customs, and respect for the Roman gods. Physical education and training were also important as the ancient Romans expected their young citizens to be prepared to serve and, if necessary, fight in the army.

Most boys of wealthy Roman families were educated in schools away from the home, while boys from poorer Roman families were educated at home by their fathers. Roman boys who did go to school went seven days a week—there were no days off at the weekend. But they would get a day off when there was a religious festival or celebration.

For recreation, Roman boys played at war, using wooden swords. They played board games, walked on stilts, flew kites, and made models. They also played with hobby horses and hoops.

When a Roman boy reached adulthood sometime between the ages of 14 and 17, he was entitled to wear the pure white toga of a man and Roman citizen.

The Romans used to clean themselves with olive oil since they did not have any soap. They would pour the oil on their bodies, and then use a strigil, a type of blade, to scrape off any dirt along with the oil.

PRIVY MATTERS

Some Roman toilets had seats with basins underneath that emptied into the sewer system. In rare buildings there was evidence of a cistern above the seats, so that the toilet could be flushed. As far as public facilities were concerned, urinal pots and public toilets served the public need. Public toilets—rectangular-shaped rooms, some seating up to one hundred people—contained rows of long stone benches, each with a row of keyhole-shaped openings cut into it. Water running down drains underneath the benches would flush waste away into the sewers. Sponge-sticks were used instead of toilet paper.

Urine from men's public urinals was sold as a commodity. Fullers (the Roman version of a dry cleaner) would empty the urinal pots and use the ammonia-rich urine for laundering and bleaching togas and tunics. Ancient Romans at one time used human urine as an ingredient in their toothpaste and as a hair product.

I'M A SLAVE FOR YOU

Slaves are thought to have constituted up to 40 percent of the Roman population.

The slaves' standard sales contract stated that they were "non-returnable, except for epilepsy."

Slaves generally came from conquered peoples, but even a free man unable to pay back his debts could be sold into slavery.

Spartacus was an escaped Roman slave who led an army of 90,000 escaped slaves against the might of the Romans. He was eventually defeated and killed in 72 BC.

ILL TREATMENT

Romans used to believe that walnuts could cure head ailments, since their shape was similar to that of a brain.

Romans, in the third century, believed that the lemon was an antidote for all poisons.

One Roman "cure" for stomachache was to wash their feet and then drink the water. Another was to swallow a small amount of lead, which would cure their stomachache but could also kill them.

CHEF'S TABLE

Some Roman dishes were extremely exotic and included teats from a sow's udder, or lamb's womb stuffed with sausage meat. A recipe survives for a platter of small songbirds in asparagus sauce.

Roman emperors ate flamingo tongues, which were considered a delicacy. They also feasted on parrotfish livers, baked dormice, pheasant brains, badgers' earlobes, and wolves' nipples.

Asparagus was so prized a delicacy in ancient Rome that the emperors kept special boats to fetch it.

The Romans were as fond of "fast food" and "snack food" as modern people are. Thousands of corner food shops and taverns served food and wine in ancient Rome. People would buy food on the way to and from the games, and, sometimes, animals that had been slaughtered in the games were quickly cooked and served to the Romans—this included giraffe and lion meat.

AD SPACE

FALSE ADVERTISING

The Dairy Association's successful "Got milk?" campaign prompted them to extend their advertising to Mexico. They discovered the Spanish translation was "Are you lactating?"

Coors translated its slogan "Turn it loose" into Spanish, where it was read as "Suffer from diarrhea."

Clairol introduced the Mist Stick, a curling iron, into Germany only to find out that *mist* is slang for manure.

When Gerber started selling baby food in Africa, they used the same packaging as in the United States, with a smiling baby on the label. Later, they learned that, in Africa, companies routinely put pictures of what's inside on the labels, since many people can't read.

When American Airlines wanted to advertise its new first-class leather seats in the Mexican market, it translated its "Fly in leather" campaign literally, which meant "Fly naked" (*vuela en cuero*) in Spanish.

Colgate introduced a toothpaste in France called Cue, the name of a notorious porno magazine.

An American T-shirt maker in Miami printed shirts for the Spanish market promoting the pope's visit, but, instead of "I saw the pope" (*el Papa*), the shirts read "I saw the potato" (*la papa*).

Pepsi's "Come alive with the Pepsi generation" slogan translated into "Pepsi brings your ancestors back from the grave" in Chinese.

The Coca-Cola name in China was first read as *Kekoukela*, meaning "bite the wax tadpole" or "female horse stuffed with wax," depending on the dialect. Coke then researched forty thousand characters to find a phonetic equivalent *kokou kole*, which translated as "happiness in the mouth."

American chicken-man Frank Perdue's slogan "It takes a tough man to make a tender chicken" got terribly mangled in a Spanish translation. A photo of Perdue with one of his birds appeared on billboards all over Mexico with the caption "It takes a hard man to make a chicken aroused."

When Parker pens marketed a ballpoint pen in Mexico, its ads were supposed to read, "It won't leak in your pocket and embarrass you." The company mistranslated the word "embarrass" as *embarazar* (to impregnate), so the ad read: "It won't leak in your pocket and make you pregnant."

Toyota renamed their MR2 model "MR" in France, because they feared that, if the French pronounced MR2 quickly, it could sound like "Toyota *merdeux*" ("is terrible").

The American slogan for Salem cigarettes—"Salem—feeling free"—was translated in the Japanese market as "When smoking Salem, you feel so refreshed that your mind seems to be free and empty."

Ford had a problem in Brazil when the Pinto car flopped. When the company found out that Pinto was Brazilian slang for "tiny male genitals," they pried the nameplates off and substituted Corcel, which means "horse."

When Vicks first introduced its cough drops to the German market, they were irritated to learn that the German pronunciation of "v" is "f "—which in German is the guttural equivalent of "sexual penetration." Not to be outdone, Puffs tissues tried to introduce its product, only to learn that *puff* in German is a colloquial term for a whorehouse.

Chrysler Corporation built a compact Plymouth that they named the Volare, presumably "to fly" in Italian, as that was a popular song at the time. Someone in the body-styling division decided, without consultation apparently, that an accent mark looked good on the "e." With that change, in Spanish it *could* mean "I will fly," but it could also be translated as "I will explode."

"Body by Fisher," boasted the auto giant General Motors. "Corpse by Fisher" was how the Belgians read it.

Bacardi concocted a fruity drink with the name Pavian to suggest French chic . . . but *pavian* means baboon in German.

When Otis Engineering took part in an exhibition in Moscow, a translator somehow managed to render a "completion equipment" sign into "equipment for orgasms."

The Jolly Green Giant brand translated into Arabic means "intimidating green ogre."

A famous drug company marketed a new remedy in the United Arab Emirates and used pictures to avoid any mistakes. The first picture was of someone ill, the next picture showed the person taking the medication, the last picture showed them looking well. What they forgot is that in the Arab world people read from right to left.

Japan's second-largest tourist agency was mystified when it entered English-speaking markets and began receiving requests for unusual sex tours. When they found out why, the owners of Kinki Nippon Tourist Company changed its name.

Microsoft Mouse was translated into Italian as "Micro tender rat" on the instruction sheet for a Taiwanese Microsoft-compatible mouse.

MEMORABLE SLOGANS

Scandinavian vacuum manufacturer Electrolux used the following advertisement in an American campaign: "Nothing sucks like an Electrolux."

In an effort to boost orange juice sales in England, a campaign was devised to extol the drink's eye-opening, pick-me-up qualities. Hence, the slogan "Orange juice. It gets your pecker up."

AS SEEN IN THE CLASSIFIEDS

Auto Repair Service. Free pick-up and delivery. Try us once, you'll never go anywhere again.

Our experienced Mom will care for your child. Fenced yard, meals and smacks included.

Dog for sale: eats anything and is fond of children.

Man wanted to work in dynamite factory. Must be willing to travel.

Three-year-old teacher needed for preschool. Experience preferred.

Mixing bowl set designed to please a cook with round bottom for efficient beating.

Girl wanted to assist magician in cutting-off-head illusion. Blue Cross and salary.

Dinner Special—Turkey $2.35; Chicken or Beef $2.25; Children $2.00.

READ THE DIRECTIONS

On an American Airlines packet of nuts— INSTRUCTIONS: OPEN PACKET, EAT NUTS.

On the label of a British children's cough medicine— DO NOT DRIVE A CAR OR OPERATE MACHINERY.

On the label of a British bread pudding—PRODUCT WILL BE HOT AFTER HEATING.

On the label of the Nytol sleeping aid— WARNING: MAY CAUSE DROWSINESS.

On a packet of British peanuts—WARNING: CONTAINS NUTS.

On a Sears hair dryer—DO NOT USE WHILE SLEEPING.

On a packet of Sun-Maid raisins—WHY NOT TRY TOSSING OVER YOUR FAVORITE BREAKFAST CEREAL?

On a Swanson frozen dinner—SERVING SUGGESTION: DEFROST.

On the bottom of the box of a British tiramisu dessert—DO NOT TURN UPSIDE DOWN.

DISTURBING DIAGNOSES

PERHAPS THE DOCTOR WAS MISTAKEN . . .

She has no rigors or shaking chills, but her husband states she was very hot in bed last night.

Patient has chest pain if she lies on her left side for over a year.

The patient was examined, X-rated, and sent home.

On the second day, the knee was better, and on the third day it disappeared.

The patient is tearful and crying constantly. She also appears to be depressed.

The patient has been depressed since she began seeing me in 1993.

Discharge status: Alive but without my permission.

Healthy appearing decrepit 69-year-old male, mentally alert but forgetful.

The patient refused autopsy.

The patient has no previous history of suicides.

Patient has left white blood cells at another hospital.

Patient had waffles for breakfast and anorexia for lunch.

She is numb from her toes down.

The skin was moist and dry.

The baby was delivered, the cord clamped and cut, and handed to the pediatrician, who breathed and cried immediately.

Occasional, constant, infrequent headaches.

The patient lives at home with his mother, father, and pet turtle, who is presently enrolled in day care three times a week.

Patient's past medical history has been remarkably insignificant with only a 40-pound weight gain in the past three days.

The pelvic examination will be done later on the floor.

Patient was released to outpatient department without dressing.

The patient expired on the floor uneventfully.

Patient was alert and unresponsive.

Examination reveals a well-developed male lying in bed with his family in no distress.

Rectal examination revealed a normal-size thyroid.

She stated that she had been constipated for most of her life until she got a divorce.

I saw your patient today, who is still under our car for physical therapy.

Both breasts are equal and reactive to light and accommodation.

Examination of genitalia reveals that he is circus sized.

The lab test indicated abnormal lover function.

The patient was to have a bowel resection. However, he took a job as a stockbroker instead.

Skin: Somewhat pale but present.

Patient was seen in consultation by Dr. Blank, who felt we should sit on the abdomen and I agree.

Large brown stool ambulating in the hall.

Patient has two teenage children, but no other abnormalities.

By the time he was admitted, his rapid heart had stopped, and he was feeling better.

I have suggested that he loosen his pants before standing, and then, when he stands with the help of his wife, they should fall to the floor.

The patient will need disposition, and therefore we will get Dr. Blank to dispose of him.

She slipped on the ice and apparently her legs went in separate directions in early December.

Coming from Detroit, this man has no children.

The patient experienced sudden onset of severe shortness of breath with a picture of acute pulmonary edema at home while having sex, which gradually deteriorated in the emergency room.

The patient was in his usual state of good health until his airplane ran out of gas and crashed.

Since she can't get pregnant with her husband, I thought you would like to work her up.

Many years ago, the patient had frostbite of the right shoe.

The bugs that grew out of her urine were cultured in Casualty and are not available. I WILL FIND THEM!!!

The patient left the hospital feeling much better except for her original complaints.

When she fainted, her eyes rolled around the room.

CROWN JEWELS

WHAT'S IN A NAME?

Every British queen named Jane has either been murdered, imprisoned, gone mad, died young, or been dethroned.

Prince Philip, the duke of Edinburgh, names his dogs after orchestral conductors.

The movie *The Madness of King George III* was released in America under the title *The Madness of King George*, because it was believed that American moviegoers would believe it to be a sequel, and not go see it because they had not seen *The Madness of King George I* and *II*.

King Charles VII, who was assassinated in 1167, was the first Swedish king with the name of Charles—the first six never existed. Almost 300 years went before there was a Charles VIII.

ROYAL MESSES

The reign of Tsar Nicholas II of Russia ended in tragedy in 1918, when he and his family were murdered, but it had started badly as well. At his coronation, presents were given to all the people who attended. But a rumor started that there weren't enough to go around and, in the stampede that followed, hundreds of women and children were killed.

> Queen Supayalat of Burma ordered about 100 of her husband's relatives clubbed to death to ensure he had no contenders for the throne.

BLOWING SMOKE

Sir Walter Raleigh supposedly financed his trip to America to cultivate tobacco by betting Queen Elizabeth I that he could weigh the weight of smoke. He did it by placing two identical cigars on opposite sides of a scale, lighting one and making sure no ashes fell. The difference in the weight after the cigar was finished was the weight of smoke—so Raleigh was on his way to America.

> After Sir Walter Raleigh introduced tobacco into England in the early seventeenth century, King James I wrote a booklet against smoking.

HARSH TASKMASTERS

Tsar Peter the Great made Russian peasants dig the foundations of St. Petersburg with their bare hands.

King Edward VII was so enthusiastic about his hunting that he arranged for all of the 180 or so clocks on the Sandringham Estate to be set a half hour early to allow him more time for his sport. Anyone having business with the king needed to ensure that they kept their appointment to "Sandringham time." George V maintained this same tradition throughout his reign; however, when Edward VIII took the throne in 1936, he arranged for all of the clocks to be reset and kept in line with those in the rest of his kingdom.

King Alfonso of Spain was so tone-deaf that he had one man in his employ known as the "Anthem Man," whose duty was to tell the king to stand up whenever the Spanish national anthem was played, because the monarch couldn't recognize it.

Tsar Paul I of Russia banished soldiers to Siberia for marching out of step.

HER MAJESTIES

Mary Stuart became queen of Scotland when she was only six days old.

When Elizabeth I of Russia died in 1762, fifteen thousand dresses were found in her closets. She used to change what she was wearing two or even three times an evening.

Queen Elizabeth II was an 18-year-old mechanic in the

English military during World War II. She was *Time* magazine's Man of the Year in 1952.

> Queen Lydia Liliuokalani was the last reigning monarch of the Hawaiian Islands. She was also the only queen the United States ever had.

Queen Anne assigned her reportedly cross-dressing cousin Lord Cornbury to the post of governor of New York and New Jersey in 1701.

> The Spanish kingdom of Castile once had a reigning queen who had been a nun. She was Doña Urraca of the house of Navarre, daughter of Alfonso the VI of Leon and Castile, and reigned from 1109 to 1126. She eventually married and had a son, who took the throne when she died.

Catherine the Great of Russia relaxed by being tickled.

⬟ BATHING BEAUTIES

Queen Elizabeth I regarded herself as a paragon of cleanliness. She declared that she bathed once every three months, whether she needed it or not.

In her entire lifetime, Queen Isabella of Spain bathed twice.

HIS HIGHNESSES

In 1974, Cairo Museum Egyptologists, noticing that the mummy of Pharaoh Ramses II was rapidly deteriorating, decided to fly it to Paris for examination. The mummy was issued an Egyptian passport that listed his occupation as "King (deceased)." According to a Discovery Channel documentary, the mummy was received at a Paris airport with the full military honors befitting a king.

King George I of England could not speak English. He was born and raised in Germany and never learned to speak English even though he was king from 1714 to 1727. He left the running of the country to his ministers, thereby creating the first government cabinet.

In the fourteenth century, King Edward II was deposed in favor of his son, Edward III, and later killed. It is rumored that in order not to mark his body, and hide evidence of murder, a deer horn was inserted into his rectum and a red hot poker was placed inside that. His ghostly screams are said to still be heard in the castle.

King Louis the XIV, also known as the Sun King, was rumored not to be the son of Louis the XIII, but the son of a Danish nobleman who served in France as a general and *marechal* of France. Supposedly he had to leave France when the boy grew up, because Louis was his spitting image.

King Louis XV was the first person to use an elevator; in 1743, his "flying chair" carried him between floors of the Versailles Palace.

> If the arm of King Henry I had been 42 inches long, the unit of measure of a foot today would be 14 inches. But his arm happened to be 36 inches long, and he decreed that the "standard" foot should be one-third that length, or 12 inches.

SIMPLY SUPERSTITIONS

BETTER SAFE THAN SORRY

You will have bad luck if you don't get out of bed on the same side that you got in.

Wear a blue bead to protect yourself from witches.

It is bad luck to place a hat on the bed.

It is bad luck to turn a loaf of bread upside down once a slice has been removed.

Leaving a house by a different door than the one you used on entry brings bad luck.

A necklace of amber beads protects against illness and colds.

It is bad luck to take a broom with you when you move. Always throw out the old and buy a new one.

Make a wish if you meet a chimney sweep by chance and it will come true.

You can avoid headaches for the year to come by having your hair cut on Good Friday.

Letting milk boil over brings bad luck.

Saying the word "pig" while fishing at sea brings bad luck.

If you catch a falling leaf in autumn, you won't get a cold all winter.

Seeing an owl in sunlight is bad luck.

Planting rosemary by the front door keeps witches away.

A wish made when you see a shooting star will come true.

If you knit some of your own hairs into a garment, then the recipient will be bound to you.

Mirrors should be covered during a thunderstorm as they attract lightning.

When you sneeze, place a hand in front of your mouth to prevent your soul escaping.

It is bad luck to open an umbrella indoors, especially if you put it over your head.

It is bad luck to count the cars in a funeral cortege.

It is bad luck to wear opals unless you were born in October.

All windows should be opened the moment someone dies so their soul can leave.

It is very bad luck to wear something new to a funeral, especially new shoes.

To bring luck, the first gift a bride opens should be the first gift she uses.

An acorn carried in your pocket brings good luck and long life.

It is bad luck to let a flag touch the ground.

Spitting on a new cricket bat before using it makes it lucky.

Mirrors in a house with a corpse should be covered or a person who sees himself will die next.

A knife placed under the bed during childbirth will ease the pain of labor.

A raw onion cut in half and placed under a sick person's bed will draw off fever and poisons.

Use the same pencil for a test as you use to study for it and it will remember the answers.

Putting salt on the doorstep of a new house stops evil from entering.

An acorn on the windowsill will prevent lightning striking.

It is unlucky to see your face in a mirror by candle-light.

To know the number of children you will have, cut an apple in half and count the number of pips.

You must hold your breath when walking past a cemetery or you will breathe in the spirit of someone who recently died.

If you sweep out the room occupied by an unwelcome guest, then it will prevent their returning.

It is bad luck to step on a crack in the pavement.

Ivy on the walls of a house protects the occupants from witches and evil spirits.

It is bad luck to kill a ladybird.

It is bad luck to spill salt, unless you throw a pinch of it over your left shoulder, into the face of the devil waiting there.

FEELING OMEN-OUS

When cows lift their tails, it is a sign that rain is on the way.

If you bid farewell to a friend while standing on a bridge, you will never see each other again.

If you dream of fish, then someone you know is pregnant.

An itch in your right palm means you will soon be receiving money. An itch in the left palm means you will be soon paying money out.

A bird entering the house is a sign of death.

Crossed knives on a table mean a quarrel.

A major row with your best friend will follow if you spill pepper.

If you drop a pair of scissors, then your lover is being unfaithful.

When three people are photographed together, the one in the middle will die first.

If a dead person's eyes are left open, he will find someone to take with him.

If you bite your tongue while eating, it shows you have recently told a lie.

If you dream of death it's a sign of birth, and if you dream of birth it's a sign of death.

The person who gives the third wedding gift to be opened by a bride will soon have a baby.

If the groom drops the wedding ring during the wedding ceremony, the marriage is doomed.

A black cat walking toward you brings good luck. Walking away from you, it takes the luck with it.

Seeing a black cat or a chimney sweep on the way to a wedding is very lucky.

If a girl sleeps with a piece of a friend's wedding cake under her pillow, she will dream of her future husband.

If a swarm of bees nests in the roof, it means the house will burn down.

Dropping an umbrella on the floor means there will be a murder in the house.

Thunder immediately following a funeral means the dead person's soul has reached heaven.

If the first butterfly you see in a year is white, then you will have good luck all year.

If your right ear itches, someone is speaking well of

you. If your left ear itches, they are speaking badly of you.

A woman buried in black will return to haunt the family.

Seeing an ambulance is very unlucky unless you hold your breath or pinch your nose until you see a black or brown dog.

Starting a trip on a Friday means you will meet misfortune.

UNIVERSALLY KNOWN

UNIVERSAL MATTERS

Based on various cosmological techniques, the universe is estimated at about 13.7 billion years old, give or take about 200 million years. Put another way, if the years flashed by at a rate of one each second, the universe would already be about 47 years old.

Scientists believe that hydrogen comprises approximately 90 to 99 percent of all matter in the universe.

It is estimated by scientists that the universe contains 0.000000000000000000000000000001 grams of matter per cubic centimeter of space. It is also estimated that the observable universe is 92 to 94 billion light years in diameter (if the observable universe is considered a sphere). Interestingly, it is possible that the universe is actually *smaller* than the observable universe. What is assumed to be very distant galaxies could in fact be duplicate images of other nearby galaxies created by light that has circumnavigated the universe. However, this is a difficult hypothesis to test because different images of a galaxy would show various time frames in its history, and therefore might appear dissimilar.

🌰 GALAXY QUEST

It is estimated that, within the entire universe, there are more than a trillion galaxies.

Galaxies come in many different shapes, which are determined by the effects of past gravitational encounters with other galaxies. Our Milky Way is a spiral-type galaxy. Three-quarters of the galaxies in the universe are spiral galaxies. There are three other types of galaxies: elliptical, irregular, and lenticular.

The Milky Way galaxy is about 100,000 light-years in diameter, and our sun is estimated to be 26,100 light-years from the center. Our solar system lies halfway along the Orion arm of the Milky Way.

If you drove a car from Earth at a constant speed of 100 miles an hour, it would take about 221,000 million years to reach the center of the Milky Way. Yet our galaxy is minute compared to the radio galaxies being discovered at the edge of the known universe.

The Milky Way probably contains millions of old neutron stars that have stopped spinning, and so are undetectable.

Most scientists agree that there is likely a supermassive black hole at the center of our galaxy, weighing as much as 4 million suns. The black hole may be capturing stars, gas, and dust equivalent to the weight of three Earths every year.

The Swedish Solar System is the world's largest scale model of the solar system.

A galaxy of typical size—about 100 billion stars—produces less energy than a single quasar.

The Andromeda galaxy is the largest member of our local group of galaxies. The Milky Way is second largest in this group. The Andromeda galaxy is the most distant object visible to the naked eye. It is about 12 billion billion miles away.

MOON MYSTERIES

The moon is about 238,000 miles away from Earth. At that distance, it is Earth's closest neighbor. Light from the moon takes about a second and a half to reach Earth.

The moon is about two-thirds as wide as the United States: 2,160 miles.

The moon weighs 81 billion tons.

Scientists have determined that most rocks on the surface of the moon are between 3 and 4.6 billion years old.

The moon orbits Earth every 27.32 days.

The dark spots on the moon that create the benevolent "man in the moon" image are actually basins filled three to eight kilometers deep with basalt, a dense mineral, which causes immense gravitational variations.

The temperature on the moon reaches 243°F at midday on the lunar equator. During the night, the temperature falls to −261°F.

Plenilune is an archaic term for a full moon.

The moon is 1 million times drier than the Gobi Desert.

The moon has about 3 trillion craters larger than three feet in diameter.

Mare Tranquillitatis, or Sea of Tranquillity, was the name of the basin on the first manned lunar landing. The Sea of Tranquillity is not a real sea, but a "maria," one of the regions on the moon that appear dark when looking at it.

The largest moon crater visible from Earth is called Bailly, or the "fields of ruin." It covers an area of about 26,000 square miles, about three times the size of Wales.

The moon does not have a global magnetic field.

The point in a lunar orbit that is farthest from the moon is called an apolune.

At the end of every 19 years, the lunar phases repeat themselves. In effect, the tide tables for the next 19 years will be approximately the same as those for the past 19 years.

Selenologists are those who study the moon.

Arthur C. Clarke, in 1959, made a bet that the first man to land on the moon would do so by June 1969. U.S. astronauts landed on July 20, 1969.

About 50 seconds' worth of fuel remained when *Apollo 11*'s lunar module landed on the moon.

The footprints left by the Apollo astronauts will not erode since there is no wind or water on the moon and should last at least 10 million years.

The size of the first footprint on the moon was 13 by 6 inches, the dimensions of Neil Armstrong's boot when he took his historic walk.

When the *Apollo 12* astronauts landed on the moon, the impact caused the moon's surface to vibrate for 55 minutes. The vibrations were picked up by laboratory instruments, leading geologists to theorize that the moon's surface is composed of fragile layers of rock.

The multilayered space suit worn by astronauts on the Apollo moon landings weighed 180 pounds on Earth and 30 pounds on the moon with the reduced lunar gravity.

Even though there were only six manned lunar landings, there are seven *Apollo* lunar landers on the moon. *Apollo 10*, as part of their mission, dropped their lunar lander to test seismic equipment that had already been set up on a previous mission.

The first spacecraft to send back pictures of the far side of the moon was *Luna 3* in October 1959. The photographs covered about 70 percent of the far side.

The final resting place for Dr. Eugene Shoemaker is the moon. The famed U.S. Geological Survey astronomer had trained the Apollo mission astronauts about craters, but never made it into space. Dr. Shoemaker had wanted to be an astronaut but was rejected because of a medical problem. His ashes were placed on board the *Lunar Prospector* spacecraft before it was launched on January 6, 1998. NASA crashed the probe into a crater on the moon on July 31, 1999, in an attempt to learn if there is water on the moon.

SOLELY SOLAR

The sun is about 300,000 times larger than the Earth. The weight of the sun is estimated at 2 billion billion billion tons, about 333,420 times that of the Earth.

The sun's surface area is 12,000 times that of Earth.

The sun contains over 99.8 percent of the total mass in our solar system, while Jupiter contains most of the rest. The fractional percentage that is left is made up of our Earth and moon and the remaining planets and asteroids.

The sun is a near-perfect sphere.

The sun is 93 million miles from Earth, yet it is 270,000 times closer than the next nearest star. It takes 8.5 minutes for light to get from the sun to Earth.

Although the sun is 400 times larger than the moon, it appears the same size in the sky because it is 400 times farther away.

The sun's equator is 2.7 million miles around; it would take 3.6 billion people holding hands to go around it.

The sun is nearly 600 times bigger than all the planets combined.

An area of the sun's surface the size of a postage stamp shines with the power of 1.5 million candles.

The sun produces more energy every minute than all the energy used on Earth in a whole year. Because it is pouring energy out into space so rapidly, the sun is shedding weight equivalent to that of a million elephants every second.

At its center, the sun has a density of over 100 times that of water. The pressure at the center of the sun is about 700 million tons per square inch. It's enough to smash atoms, expose the inner nuclei and allow them to smash into each other, interact, and produce the radiation that gives off light and warmth. The sun has a core temperature of 154 million degrees Kelvin. If a pin was heated to the same temperature as the center of the sun, its heat would set alight everything within 60 miles of it.

The sun's mass decreases by 4 million tons per second due to conversion of hydrogen to helium by thermonuclear reaction; this conversion will continue for approximately another 5 to 6 billion years before the sun's hydrogen supply is exhausted and it enters its red giant phase.

All the coal, oil, gas, and wood on Earth would keep the sun burning for only a few days.

A spectroheliokinematograph is a special camera used to film the sun.

A sunbeam setting out through space at the rate of 186,000 miles a second would describe a gigantic circle and return to its origins after about 200 billion years.

Ancient Chinese astronomers first observed sunspots about 2,000 years ago. Westerners took quite a while to catch up, first writing of the dark blotches 1,700 years later, and wrongly believing them to be small planets. The smallest visible sunspots have an area of 500 million square miles, about 50 times the size of Africa. The largest sunspots have an area of about 7,000 million square miles.

The energy released in one hour by a single sunspot is equal to all the electrical power that will be used in the United States over the next million years.

The most ancient report of a solar eclipse is in Chinese records. The eclipse came without warning, according to legend, because the royal astronomers, Hsi and Ho, were too drunk to make the necessary computations. They were executed—the only astronomers known to have been killed for dereliction of duty.

There is a correspondence between the fluctuation of

agricultural production and sunspot variations. Production of wheat, for example, reached high figures during sunspot maximums and low figures during sunspot minimums.

Giant flames called prominences shoot out from the sun's surfaces for 310,000 miles, more than the distance from Earth to the moon. The entire Earth could fit into one of these flames nearly 40 times.

The sun gives off a stream of electrically charged particles called the solar wind. Every second the sun pumps more than a million tons of material into the solar wind. The solar wind flows past Earth at 1,200 times the speed of sound.

The sun's solar wind is so powerful it has large effects on the tails of comets, and scientists have determined that it even has measurable effects on the trajectories of spacecraft.

A cosmic year is the amount of time it takes the sun to revolve around the center of the Milky Way, about 225 million years.

Galileo became totally blind shortly before his death, probably because of the damage done to his eyes during his many years of looking at the sun through a telescope.

Copernicus's book, which suggested that the sun and not the Earth was the center of the solar system, was officially banned by the papacy until 1835.

SPACE TRAVELERS

Space dust is extremely small—smaller than a particle of smoke—and widely separated, with more than 320 feet between particles.

In the twentieth century, two objects hit the Earth's surface with enough force to destroy a medium-size city. By pure luck, both landed in sparsely populated Siberia.

The average meteor, though brilliantly visible in the nighttime sky, is no larger than a grain of sand. Even the largest and brightest meteors, known as fireballs, rarely exceed the size of a pea.

More than 20 million meteoroids enter Earth's atmosphere every day.

Millions of meteorites fall against the outer limits of the atmosphere every day and are burned to nothing by the friction.

It has been estimated that at least a million meteors have hit the Earth's land surface, which is only 25 percent of the planet. Every last trace of more than 99 percent of the craters thus formed has vanished, erased by wind, water, and living things.

Five times as many meteors can be seen after midnight as can seen before.

The heaviest known meteorite to fall to Earth—the Hoba West meteorite—lies where it fell in Africa. Weighing about 60 tons, it is not likely to be moved.

Liquid water was found inside a 4.5-billion-year-old meteorite in 1999, giving scientists their first look at extra-terrestrial water.

As of 2007 the present rate of discovery of asteroids in the solar system is about 5,000 per month.

More than 100,000 asteroids lie in a belt between Mars and Jupiter.

The largest asteroid on record is Ceres. It is so big it would stretch a distance of over 600 miles. It was also the first asteroid to be discovered.

The brightest asteroid is called Vesta. It has a diameter of 335 miles and is the only asteroid visible to the unaided eye. The Hubble Space Telescope recently discovered a huge 295-mile-wide crater on Vesta. This is massive when compared to Vesta's 335-mile diameter. If Earth had a crater of proportional size, it would fill most of the Pacific Ocean basin.

In 1937 the tiny asteroid Hermes passed uncomfortably close to the Earth, at a distance of less than twice that of the moon. Astronomers later discovered that in 1942 it passed even closer. On March 23, 1989, a thousand-foot-wide asteroid missed impacting the Earth by only 400,000 miles, passing through the exact position the Earth was in six hours before. If it had hit the Earth, the resulting explosion would have been the largest in recorded history. And in 2002, *another* asteroid missed impacting the Earth by only 75,000 miles, or one-third the distance to the moon. Astronomers did not even discover the near-impact until three days later.

The word comet comes from the Greek *komé*, meaning "hair of the head." Aristotle first used the deviation *kometes*, meaning "stars with hairs."

In the history of the solar system, 30 billion comets have been lost or destroyed. That amounts to only 30 percent of the estimated number that remain.

There is now evidence that comets are propelled into the inner solar system by the tidal pull of the entire galaxy rather than by the pull of passing stars, as many astronomers had believed. And, just as the moon pulls the Earth's oceans upward on a regular, predicable timetable, the galaxy's pull on comets also follows a predictable pattern, causing greatly increased comet activity about once every 35 million years.

Until the mid-sixteenth century, comets were believed to be not astronomical phenomena, but burning vapors that had arisen from distant swamps and were propelled across the sky by fire and light.

In the sixteenth and seventeenth centuries, some people thought comets were the eggs or sperm of planetary systems.

Comets speed up as they approach the sun— sometimes reaching speeds of over 1 million miles per hour. Far away from the sun, speeds drop, perhaps down to as little as 700 miles an hour.

The tails of comets generally point away from the sun, whether the comet is approaching the sun or receding. The tail of a comet can extend 90 million miles—nearly the distance between the Earth and the sun.

The jets of water vapor discharged by a comet have a rocketlike effect. They alter the comet's orbit enough to make its course unpredictable.

If one were to capture and bottle a comet's 10,000-mile vapor trail, the amount of vapor actually present in the bottle would take up less than one cubic inch of space.

The huge halo of comets that surrounds our solar system is called the Oort Cloud.

Halley's Comet, one of the most famous comets, returns to Earth every 76 years, and has been observed and recorded for more than three thousand years. Halley's

Comet is named after Edmond Halley, who was the first to suggest that comets were natural phenomena of our solar system, in orbit around the sun.

In 1066, Halley's Comet appeared shortly before William the Conqueror invaded England. The Norman king took it as a good omen; his battle cry became "A new star, a new king."

The nucleus of Halley's Comet is a peanut-shaped object, weighing about 100,000 million tons and measuring about nine miles by five miles.

In 1994, the comet Shoemaker-Levy 9 broke apart and plunged into Jupiter, ripping holes the size of Earth in the planet's atmosphere.

PLANETARIUM

The reflecting power of a planet or satellite, expressed as a ratio of reflected light to the total amount falling on the surface, is called the albedo.

Gold exists on Mars, Mercury, and Venus.

The existence of Mercury has been known since about the third millennium BC. The planet was given two names by the Greeks: Apollo, for its apparition as a morning star, and Hermes as an evening star. Greek astronomers knew, however, that the two names referred to the same body.

A solar day on Mercury, from sunrise to sunset, lasts about six Earth months or 176 Earth days. The big time difference is due to Mercury's length of rotation, which is much slower than the Earth's. A day on Mercury is twice as long as its year. Mercury rotates very slowly but revolves around the sun in slightly less than 88 days.

Mariner 10 was the first spacecraft to fly by Mercury. In 1974, it sent back close-up pictures of a world that resembles our moon.

Temperature variations on Mercury are the most extreme in the solar system, ranging from 90°K (Kelvin) to 700°K. At midday on Mercury, the sunlight is hot enough to melt lead. The surface of Venus is actually hotter than Mercury's, despite being nearly twice as far from the sun. Lead melts at 662°F, and the surface can reach temperatures of 864°F.

The Venus day is also longer than the Venus year. The planet spins on its axis once every 243 Earth days and orbits the sun once every 224 Earth days.

The winds of Venus blow steadily at 109 miles an hour.

Carbon dioxide makes up 97 percent of Venus's atmosphere.

The diameter of Venus is only about 400 miles less than that of the Earth.

Venus, Earth's nearest planetary neighbor, at its closest to us, is 105 times farther away than our moon.

The oldest features on Venus appear to be no older than 800 million years.

Venus is much brighter than any other planet. At its brightest, it can cast shadow, and even be seen during the daytime.

The surface of Venus—millions of miles away and hidden by clouds of sulphuric acid—has been better mapped than the Earth's seabed.

Venus has no magnetic field, perhaps because of its slow rotation. It also has no satellites, though in the distant past it may have had a moon.

Venus does not tilt as it goes around the sun, so it has no seasons. On Mars, however, the seasons are more exaggerated and last much longer than on Earth.

🌰 EARTHLY DELIGHTS

Light takes one-tenth of a second to travel from New York to London, eight minutes to reach the Earth from the Sun, and 4.3 years to reach the Earth from the nearest star.

The Earth is the densest planet in the solar system.

The Earth orbits the sun at 18.5 miles a second.

Aristarchus, a Greek astronomer living about 200 BC, was reportedly the first person to declare that the Earth revolved around the sun. His theory was disregarded for hundreds of years.

Less than 50 percent of American adults understand that the Earth orbits the sun yearly, according to a basic science survey.

The Earth moves in its 585-million-mile orbit around the sun approximately eight times faster than a bullet travels.

The Earth spins faster on its axis in September than it does in March.

The pressure at the center of the Earth is 27,000 tons per square inch. At the center of the giant planet Jupiter, the pressure is three times as great.

The Earth weighs nearly 6,588,000,000,000,000,000,000,000 tons.

If you could magnify an apple to the size of the Earth, the atoms in the original apple would each be about the size of an apple.

If the world were to become totally flat and the oceans distributed themselves evenly over the Earth's surface, the water would be approximately two miles deep at every point.

A bucket filled with earth would weigh about five times more than the same bucket filled with the substance of the sun. However, the force of gravity is so much greater on the sun that a person weighing 150 pounds on Earth would weigh 2 tons on the sun.

Without using precision instruments, Eratosthenes measured the radius of the Earth in the third century BC, and came within 1 percent of the value determined by today's technology.

The distance around Earth's equator is 24,920 miles; it would take 33 million people holding hands to reach across distance.

The world is not round. It is an oblate spheroid, flattened at the poles and bulging at the equator.

The temperature of Earth's interior increases by one degree every 60 feet down.

The first photo of Earth taken from space was shot from the *Vanguard 2* in 1959.

Earth is the only planet not named after a god.

To reach outer space, you need to travel at least 50 miles from Earth's surface.

Afternoon temperatures on Mars go up to about 80°F in some areas, and down to -190°F at night.

The largest volcano known is on Mars: Olympus Mons, 370 miles wide and 16 miles high, is almost three times higher than Mount Everest.

The moons of Mars are called Phobos and Deimos after two mythical horses that drew the chariot of Mars, the Roman god of war. Phobos is so close to its parent planet that it could not be seen by an observer standing at either of Mars's poles. Phobos makes three complete orbits around Mars every day. Deimos rises and sets twice a day.

The atmosphere of Mars is relatively moist. However, because the atmosphere is thin, the total amount of water in the atmosphere is minimal. If all the water in the atmosphere of Mars was collected, it would probably fill only a small pond.

Mars takes 1.88 years to orbit the sun, so its seasons are about twice as long as those on Earth.

Statistically, UFO sightings are at their greatest number during those times when Mars is closest to the Earth.

An object weighing 100 pounds on Earth would weigh just 38 pounds on Mars.

Antarctica was used as a testing laboratory for the joint United States–Soviet Union mission to Mars because it has much in common with the red planet.

Jupiter is the largest planet, and it has the shortest day. Although Jupiter has a circumference of 280,000 miles, compared with the Earth's 25,000 miles, Jupiter manages to make one turn in 9 hours and 55 minutes. However, its years are 12 times as long as the Earth's.

Jupiter has no solid surface, only layers of gaseous clouds. It is composed mainly of hydrogen and helium.

All the planets in our solar system could be placed inside Jupiter. Jupiter is two and a half times larger than all the other planets, satellites, asteroids, and comets of our solar system combined.

Jupiter is so big and has such a large atmosphere that many astronomers think it almost became a star.

The Great Red Spot on Jupiter is a swirling hurricane of gases. The winds in the hurricane reach 21,700 miles per hour.

Jupiter has 16 moons, the largest of which is Ganymede, which looks like a cracked eggshell. Ganymede is bigger than Mercury, the smallest planet. It is 3,275 miles in diameter.

Metis is the innermost of Jupiter's known satellites and was named after a Titaness who was the first wife of the Greek god Zeus, known later as Jupiter in Roman mythology.

Astronomers believe Jupiter's moon Europa may have an ocean of liquid water beneath an ice cap.

Jupiter's moon Adrastea is one of the smallest moons in our solar system. It measures about 12.4 miles.

There are seven rings surrounding Saturn. Each of the rings is made up of thousands of ringlets, which are made up of billions of objects of varying sizes from thirty-three-foot-wide icebergs to pinhead-small ice specks. Driving at 75 miles an hour, it would take 258 days to drive around one of Saturn's rings.

Winds ten times stronger than a hurricane on earth blow around Saturn's equator. Wind speeds can reach 1,100 miles an hour.

Titan, Saturn's largest moon, is the only moon in our solar system to have an atmosphere. However, it cannot support life as its atmosphere is made of nitrogen and methane gas.

Uranus, the seventh planet from the sun, is tipped on its side so that at any moment one pole is pointed at the sun. The polar regions are warmer than the equator. At the poles, a day lasts for 42 Earth years, followed by an equally long night.

Uranus was only discovered 225 years ago, on March 13, 1781, by Sir William Herschel.

Uranus is visible to the naked eye.

Uranus has 15 known satellites.

The discovery of Neptune was announced in 1846. But, when astronomers checked previous records, they found the record of an observation of the planet as far back as 1795 by astronomers who, believing it to be a star, recorded the position routinely. Since Neptune's discovery, it has made about three-quarters of one revolution of the sun.

Neptune is so remote that light from the sun—though traveling at 186,000 miles per second—takes more than four hours to reach the planet. By comparison, light from the sun takes only eight minutes to reach the Earth. From Neptune, the sun would only appear to be a very bright star.

Neptune is a maximum distance of 2.82 billion miles from the sun. The length of one of its days is 17 hours 6 minutes, and the length of one of its years is 165 Earth days.

Neptune has eight known satellites. The coldest place in the solar system is the surface of Neptune's largest moon Triton, which has a temperature of −391°F, only 69°F above absolute zero.

Besides Earth, only Jupiter, Saturn, Uranus, and Neptune have known magnetic fields.

The average surface temperature of Uranus, Neptune, and Pluto is about −364°F, 11 times colder than inside a home freezer.

Small satellites within a planet's rings are sometimes called "mooms."

Scientists are still finding new planets, but not in our solar system. Recently a new planet was discovered orbiting the star Epsilon Eridani, which is only 10.5 light-years from the Earth.

PLUTOPIA

In 2006, the International Astronomical Union (IAU), which decides the official names of all celestial bodies, voted overwhelmingly to change Pluto's classification from "planet" to "dwarf planet," making the official number of planets in the solar system eight. The decision came after a multiyear search for a scientific definition of "planet," which had never had an official meaning before.

Pluto takes 248 Earth years to orbit the sun. For 20 of those years, it is closer to the sun than Neptune. Because of a large orbital eccentricity, Pluto was closer to the sun than Neptune between January 1979 and March 1999. The nature of its orbit, however, always prevents it from colliding with Neptune. Some astronomers believe Pluto's strange and erratic orbit indicates that it was originally a moon of Neptune that somehow broke loose.

Traveling at the speed of 186,000 miles per second, light takes six hours to travel from Pluto to Earth.

To an observer standing on Pluto, the sun would appear no brighter than Venus appears in our evening sky.

Pluto's one moon, Charon, is 12,200 miles from the planet
and has a diameter of just 740 miles. First seen from Earth in
1978, tiny Charon is similar in size to Pluto. The two bodies orbit each other like a double planet, with the same sides per-
manently facing each other. Pluto and Charon are so close in
proximity it is believed that they may share an atmosphere.

ASTRO ANSWERS

The telescope on Mount Palomar, California, can see a
distance of 7,038,835,200,000,000,000,000 miles.

The largest number of telescopes in one city in the
world is in Tucson, Arizona.

The largest refracting telescope is the 40-inch Yerkes telescope, built in 1897 and still in use. All larger telescopes
are of the "reflecting" variety, using mirrors instead of
lenses.

A space shuttle at liftoff develops more power than
all the cars in England combined.

Neil Armstrong's training space suit brought in $178,500
at auction. This was more than double its presale estimate.

On September 21, 1978, two Soviet cosmonauts set a
space endurance record of 96 days.

When astronauts first shaved in space, their weightless
whiskers floated up to the ceiling. A special razor had to

be developed that drew the whiskers in like a vacuum cleaner.

TWINKLE, TWINKLE LITTLE STAR

In the Middle Ages, many people believed that stars were beams of light shining through the floor of heaven.

The brightness of a star is called its magnitude. The smaller the magnitude is, the brighter the star is.

When we look at the farthest visible star, we are looking 4 billion years into the past—the light from that star, traveling at 186,000 miles a second, has taken that many years to reach us.

Eighty-eight different constellations have been identified and named by astronomers.

There are 200 to 400 billion stars in the Milky Way galaxy. The sun is about midway in the scale of star sizes, but most are smaller ones. Only 5 percent of the stars in our galaxy are larger than the sun. (That's still 5 billion larger stars.)

If you attempted to count the stars in a galaxy at a rate of one every second, it would take around 3,000 years to count them all.

On a clear night, more than 2,000 stars are visible to the naked eye.

Two of every three stars in the galaxy are binary, meaning pairs of stars are more common than single-star systems like our own.

About 40 novae erupt in our galaxy each year.

A typical nova explosion releases about as much energy as the sun emits in 10,000 years, or as much as in 1^{21} nuclear bombs.

The layer of gas that spreads out from a nova explosion can travel at speeds of 5 million miles per hour.

A brown dwarf is a very small dark object, with a mass less than one-tenth that of the sun. They are "failed stars"—globules of gas that have shrunk under gravity, but failed to ignite and shine as stars.

If a red giant star was the size of an ordinary living room, its energy-generating core would be the size of the period at the end of this sentence.

It takes 100,000 years for a red giant to change into a white dwarf. By astronomical standards, this is practically instantaneous, a mere one-thousandth of the star's life.

A white dwarf has a mass equal to that of the sun, but a diameter only about that of the Earth. A cupful of white dwarf material weighs about 22 tons, the same as five elephants.

> An estimated 10,000 million stars in our galaxy have died and produced white dwarfs.

The smallest star found to date is a neutron star that has a diameter of 59 kilometers but a mass 10 times that of our sun. This star is more commonly known as a black hole.

> American physicist John Wheeler coined the term "black hole" in 1967; before this the phenomena were known as "frozen stars."

The gravitational pull of a black hole is so strong that, if a two-pound book were brought within 20 feet of a black hole, the book would weigh more than the entire world's population combined.

> A neutron star is the strongest magnet in the universe. The magnetic field of a neutron star is a million million times stronger than the Earth's magnetism.

The force of gravity is very strong on a neutron star because of its amazing density. Your weight on a neutron star would be 10,000 million times greater than on Earth. If an astronaut tried to land on a neutron star, he or she would be crushed by the extremely strong force of gravity, and squashed into a thin layer less than one atom thick.

Some neutron stars spin 600 times a second, which is as fast as a dentist's drill.

The surface temperature of a neutron star is about 1.8 million degrees Fahrenheit.

The first pulsar (a rotating neutron star that emits brief, sharp pulses of radio waves instead of the steady radiation associated with other natural sources), discovered in 1967, never varies in its timing by even as much as a hundred-millionth of a second. Its pulse is registered every 1.33730109 seconds. A pulsar's neutrons are so densely packed together that, if one the size of a nickel landed on Earth, it would weigh approximately 100 million tons.

When the first pulsar signal was detected, it was thought that its signals might be a message from an alien civilization deep in space. The signal was jokingly labeled LGM, for "little green men."

Quasars are amazingly bright objects. A quasar generates 100 times as much light as the whole of our galaxy in a space not much larger than our solar system.

A car traveling at a constant speed of 60 miles an hour would take longer than 48 million years to reach the nearest star (other than our sun), Proxima Centauri. This is about 685,000 average human lifetimes. Proxima Centauri is too small to be seen without a telescope. If you traveled to Proxima Centauri, the sun would appear to be a bright star in the constellation of Cassiopeia.

The brightest star in the night sky is Sirius. Also known as the Dog Star, it is 51 trillion miles from the Earth, or about 8.7 light-years. The second brightest star is Canopus, which is only visible in the Southern Hemisphere.

The star Alpha Herculis is 25 times larger than the circumference described by the Earth's revolution around the sun.

The star Antares is 60,000 times larger than our sun. If our sun were the size of a softball, the star Antares would be as large as a house.

The star known as LP 327-186, a so-called white dwarf, is smaller than the state of Texas, yet so dense that if a cubic inch of it were brought to Earth, it would weigh more than 1.5 million tons.

The star Sirius B is so dense, a handful of it weighs about 1 million pounds.

The star Zeta Thaun, a supernova, was so bright when it exploded in 1054 that it could be seen during the day.

In the constellation Cygnus, there is a double star, one of whose components has such a high surface gravity that light cannot escape from it. Many astronomers believe Cygnus X-1 was the first "black hole" to be detected.

Barnard's star is approaching the sun at a speed of 87 miles per second. By the year 11700, it will be the closest star to us, at a distance of about 3.8 light-years. However, because it is so dim, it will still not be visible to the naked eye.

The current North Star (the star best suited for navigation northward) is Polaris. Because the direction of Earth's axis is constantly changing, the title gets passed along every couple of centuries. The next North Star will be Gamma Cephai around AD 3000. By the year AD 14000, the North Star will be Vega.

The most luminous star is probably Eta Carinae, which has a maximum luminosity of around 4 million times that of the sun.

The giant red star Betelgeuse—the red star in the shoulder of the constellation Orion—is 700 million miles across, about 800 times larger than the sun, or more than a quarter the size of our entire solar system. Light takes one hour to travel from one side of the giant star to the other.

The dense globules of gas from which stars are born are much larger than the stars they will form. In the Orion nebula, globules have been detected that are 500 times larger than the solar system.

The Veil nebula was formed by an explosion that took place over 30,000 years ago, when the first people lived on Earth.

The Hercules global cluster is the brightest cluster in the northern sky. It was discovered by English scientist Edmond Halley in 1714.

The Tarantula nebula is the largest known nebula. It is 160,000 light-years away. If it were as close to us as the Orion nebula, its light would cast shadows on Earth. It is thought to contain a huge star of over 1,000 times the mass of the sun, 10 times more massive than any star in the Milky Way.

The coldest place in the known universe is the Boomerang Nebula, about 5,000 light-years away.

GLOBE TROTTING

SHORT BUT SWEET

The shortest place names in the United States are L, a lake in Nebraska; T, a gulch in Colorado; D, a river in Oregon flowing from Devil's Lake to the ocean; and Y, a city in Arkansas. Each is named after its shape.

In Europe, E is a river in Perthshire, Scotland; there are villages called Å in Norway, Sweden, and Denmark, and there's a Y in France.

The Pacific Caroline Islands has a place named U, and a peak in Hong Kong is called A.

WATER, WATER EVERYWHERE

Hawaii's Mount Waialeale is the wettest place in the world—it rains about 90 percent of the time, about 480 inches per year.

It is illegal to swim in Central Park, New York.

At the deepest point (6.8 miles), an iron ball would take more than an hour to sink to the ocean floor.

The largest wave ever recorded was near the Japanese Island of Ishigaki in 1971, at 279 feet high.

The surface of the Dead Sea is 1,312 feet below the surface of the Mediterranean Sea, which is only 47 miles away.

The Dead Sea is in fact an inland lake.

The water in the Dead Sea is so salty that it is far easier to float than to drown.

The volume of water in the Amazon River is greater than the next eight largest rivers in the world combined.

In 1908, the Moskva River in Russia rose 30 feet, flooding 100 streets and 2,500 houses.

The world's longest freshwater beach is located in Canada.

Over the years, the Niagara Falls have moved more than 7 miles from their original site.

The Angel Falls in Venezuela are nearly 20 times taller than Niagara Falls.

The Nile River has frozen over only twice in living memory—once in the ninth century, and then again in the eleventh century.

Rio de Janeiro translates to "River of January."

The farthest point from any ocean is in China.

The world's largest delta was created by the River Ganges.

New York City contains 572 miles of shoreline.

The East Alligator River in Australia's Northern Territory was misnamed. It contains crocodiles, not alligators.

The mythical Connla's Well, home to the Salmon of Wisdom, is the legendary source of Ireland's Shannon and Boyne Rivers.

The Atlantic Ocean covers the world's longest mountain range.

BUT NOT A DROP TO DRINK

No rain has ever been recorded falling in the Atacama Desert in Chile.

There are no rivers in Saudi Arabia.

DISASTER ZONE

Two minor earthquakes occur every minute somewhere in the world.

One of the greatest natural disasters of recent centuries occurred in 1976 when an earthquake hit Tangshan, China, killing three-quarters of a million people.

In 1992 a series of thunderstorms in southeast Queensland spawned two of the most powerful tornadoes in recorded Australian history, including the only Australian tornado to be given an F4 classification.

In 1896, Britain and Zanzibar were at war for 38 minutes.

Eighty-two percent of the workers on the Panama Canal suffered from malaria.

In May 1948, Mount Ruapehu and Mount Ngauruhoe, both in New Zealand, erupted simultaneously.

The background radiation in Aberdeen is twice that of the rest of Great Britain.

Lightning strikes the Earth about 200 times a second.

On January 15, 1867, there was a severe frost in London, and more than 40 people died in Regent's Park when the ice broke on the main lake.

COLD AS ICE

Antarctic means "opposite the Artic."

The northernmost country claiming part of Antarctica is Norway.

Underneath the great icy plains of the Antarctic, little pools of unfrozen water can sometimes be found.

It snowed in the Sahara Desert on February 18, 1979.

The largest iceberg recorded, in 1956, was 200 miles long and 60 miles wide, larger than the country of Belgium.

The Novaya Zemlya glacier in Russia is more than 250 miles long.

The coldest temperature ever recorded on Earth was −94°F in Siberia.

The Eskimo language has more than 20 words to describe different kinds of snow.

Ten percent of the salt mined in the world each year is used to de-ice the roads in America.

Dirty snow melts quicker than clean snow.

On March 30, 1867, Alaska was officially purchased from Russia for about two cents an acre. At the time, many politicians believed this purchase of "wasteland to be a costly folly."

During winter, the skating rinks in Moscow cover more than 250,000 square miles of land.

NAME GAMES

200 million years ago, the Earth contained one land mass called Pangaea.

The country of Benin changed its name from Dahomey in 1975.

Maryland was named after Queen Henrietta Maria.

Tokyo was once called Edo.

In 1825, Upper Peru became Bolivia.

The southwestern tip of the Isle of Man is called the Calf of Man.

The city of Edinburgh is nicknamed "Auld Reekie" meaning "Old Smoky."

The DC in Washington, DC, stands for District of Columbia.

The inhabitants of Monaco are known as Monegasques.

A person from the country of Nauru is called a Nauruan; this is the only palindromic nationality.

There is a town in West Virginia called Looneyville.

New York was once called New Amsterdam.

Greenland—named this to attract settlers—was discovered by Eric the Red in the tenth century.

The southernmost tip of Africa is not the Cape of Good Hope, but Cape Agulhas.

Brazil got its name from the nut, not the other way around.

Spain literally means "the land of rabbits."

Mount Everest was known as Peak 15 before being renamed after Sir George Everest, the British surveyor-general of India, in 1865.

A 453-foot-tall building in New York City is called the Lipstick Building because of its oval shape and façade of red enamel and granite. The top portion of the building is designed to appear retractable, like a lipstick.

Icelandic phone books list people by their given name, not their surname.

SIZE MATTERS

Canada is larger than China, which is larger than the United States.

The world's largest national park is Wood Buffalo National Park in Canada.

The world's largest exporter of sugar is Cuba.

England is smaller than New England. There is no point in England more than 75 miles from the ocean.

The United States, which accounts for 6 percent of the population of the world, consumes nearly 60 percent of the world's resources.

Discounting Australia, which is generally regarded as a continental landmass, the world's largest island is Greenland.

As the Pacific plate moves under its coast, the North Island of New Zealand is getting larger.

France contains the greatest length of paved roads.

There are more Samoans in Los Angeles than on American Samoa.

POPULATION GROWTH

The number of births in India each year is greater than the entire population of Australia.

The only country to register zero births in 1983 was the Vatican City.

TIME TO MAKE HISTORY

Benjamin Franklin was first to suggest daylight savings time.

Captain Cook was the first man to set foot on all continents except Antarctica.

Florida first saw the cultivation of oranges in 1539.

England's Stonehenge is 1,500 years older than Rome's Colosseum.

Numbering houses in London streets only began in 1764.

The tree on the Lebanese flag is a cedar.

There are three Great Pyramids at Giza.

The inhabitants of Papua New Guinea speak about 700 languages (including localized dialects, which are known to change from village to village), approximately 15 percent of the world's total.

The world's first national park was Yellowstone.

Sixty percent of all U.S. potato products originate in Idaho.

New York's Central Park opened in 1876.

Within a few years of Columbus's discovery of America, the Spaniards had killed 1.5 million Indians.

Hawaii officially became a part of the United States on June 14, 1900.

The Tower of London, during its lifetime, has served many purposes, including a royal menagerie.

The Tibetan mountain people use yak's milk as their form of currency.

In the Andes, time is often measured by how long it takes to smoke a cigarette.

The Spanish Inquisition once condemned the entire population of the Netherlands to death for heresy.

ART AND CRAFTS

The Incas and the Aztecs were able to function without the wheel.

Obsidian, used by American Indians for tools, weapons, and ornaments, is dark volcanic glass.

The state flag of Alaska was designed by a 13-year-old boy.

THE LAY OF THE LAND

The most abundant metal in the Earth's crust is aluminum.

More than 75 percent of all the countries in the world are north of the equator.

Less than 1 percent of the Caribbean Islands are inhabited.

Mountains are formed by a process called orogeny.

The city of Istanbul straddles two separate continents, Europe and Asia.

At the nearest point, Russia and America are less than 3 miles apart.

The Scandinavian capital of Stockholm is built on nine islands connected by bridges.

La Paz in Bolivia is so high above sea level that there is barely enough oxygen in the air to support a fire.

The Forth railway bridge in Scotland is 3 feet longer in summer than in winter, due to thermal expansion.

If you travel from east to west across the former Soviet Union, you will cross seven time zones.

In the north of Norway, the sun shines constantly for about 14 weeks each summer.

The Polynesian country of Niue is a 106-square-mile limestone rock emerging 197 feet from the Pacific.

Yugoslavia is bordered by seven other countries.

The fastest tectonic movement on Earth is 240 millimeters per year, at the Tonga microplate near Samoa.

A quarter of Russia is covered by forest.

PRECIOUS METALS

Fulgurite is formed when lightning strikes sand.

Until the eighteenth century, India produced almost all the world's diamonds.

There is about 200 times more gold in the world's oceans than has been mined in our entire history.

South Africa produces two-thirds of the world's gold.

BEING THE BEST

THE HEIGHTS OF GREATNESS

The tallest Miss America contestant, Jeanne Robertson, was 6 feet, 2 inches tall. The average height of a Miss America winner is 5 feet, 6.6 inches.

The tallest president was Abraham Lincoln at 6 feet, 4 inches.

The shortest president was James Madison at 5 feet, 4 inches.

The tallest man on record was Robert Wadlow of Illinois. He was 8 feet, 11.1 inches tall, and at the time of his death at the age of 22 he weighed 490 pounds.

The tallest woman ever recorded, Trijntje Cornelisdochter, was born in 1616 in Holland. She was 8 feet, 4 inches tall when she died aged 17 in 1633.

The tallest married couple was Anna Hanen Swan

(1846–88), and Martin Van Buren Bates (1845–1919). She was 7 feet, 5.5 inches tall, and Martin stood 7 feet, 2.5 inches when they married at the Church of St. Martin-in-the-Fields, London, on June 17, 1871.

The tallest man-made structure in the world is the CN Tower located in Toronto, Canada, at 1,815 feet.

The tallest building in Jersey City, New Jersey, is the 781-foot tower at 30 Hudson Street.

At 891 feet tall, the 1.6-mile-long Millau Bridge is the tallest road bridge in the world. It crosses the Tarn Valley, in France's Massif Central Mountains, and opened in 2004. The suspension bridge hangs on seven towers, the tallest being 1,122 feet tall. It was constructed over three years at a cost of 394 million euros.

The tallest bird alive today is the ostrich.

The tallest mammal is the giraffe.

The tallest snake is the king cobra, which can rear itself up to six feet and spread its "hood" nine inches.

The highest parachute jump ever made was on August 16, 1960, as a part of the U.S. Air Force research program, Project Excelsior. Air Force Captain Joseph W. Kittinger Jr. stepped off a platform raised to 102,800 feet over Tularosa, New Mexico, by a high-altitude balloon. To survive the altitude, Kittinger wore a pressure suit similar to those used by astronauts. After 4 minutes, 36 seconds of free fall, he reached a speed of 714 miles per hour and became the only human to break the sound barrier without being enclosed in a machine of any kind. He dropped 84,700 feet before opening his parachute, and landed safely 13 minutes, 45 seconds after jumping.

The only mammal where the female is normally taller than the male is a type of antelope called the okapi.

The perfect height for a female fashion model is 5 feet, 9.5 inches. The perfect height for a male model is 6 feet even.

In the original James Bond novels, the character Dr. No was 6 feet, 6 inches tall. The character Auric Goldfinger was only 5 feet.

In 1876 the average Western man was 5 feet, 5 inches tall, 4 inches shorter than today's average. Half of that increase, a full 2 inches on average, has been since 1960, according to the U.S. Department of Health and Human Services.

The average U.S. adult male is 5 feet, 9.1 inches, but 3.9 percent of U.S. men are 6 feet, 2 inches or taller.

The average U.S. adult female is 5 feet, 3.7 inches, but 0.7 percent of U.S. women are 5 feet, 10 inches or taller.

Tsar Peter the Great stood 6 feet, 6.75 inches tall, an incredible height for the eighteenth century.

The minimum height for a U.S. astronaut is 4 feet, 10.5 inches, and the minimum height for a U.S. space shuttle pilot is five feet, four inches. The maximum height for all U.S. space shuttle crew is 6 feet, 4 inches.

The world's tallest mountains, the Himalayas, are also the fastest growing. Their growth—about half an inch a year—is caused by the pressure exerted by two of the Earth's continental plates.

LARGE AND IN CHARGE

The largest web-footed bird is the albatross.

Toronto, Ontario, was home to the biggest swimming pool in the world in 1925. It held 2,000 swimmers, and was 300 feet by 75 feet. It is still in operation.

The Tokyo World Lanes Bowling Center is the largest bowling establishment in the world, with 252 lanes.

The West Edmonton Mall, located in Edmonton, Alberta, Canada, is the world's largest shopping mall. The mall includes 5.3 million square feet of space. There are more than 800 stores, more than 110 eating establishments, 26 movie theaters and seven attractions, including an amusement park, waterpark, minigolf, ice rink, the world's largest indoor lake, and varied sea life. The mall occupies 121 acres, and the parking can accommodate 20,000 cars. The total cost for the four phases of construction for the mall topped $2.8 billion.

The USS *Enterprise* was built in Newport, Virginia, and launched in 1960 and remains the largest warship ever built and the first nuclear-powered aircraft carrier. It is the eighth ship and the second aircraft carrier to be called *Enterprise*. At 1,123 feet long and 250 feet high, the ship is both the longest and tallest warship ever built. With a top speed over 30 knots, it is also the fastest carrier in the U.S. fleet. Weighing in at 90,000 tons, the *Big E*, as it is dubbed by sailors, is home to more than 5,000 officers and crew members.

The giant sequoia (*Sequoiadendron giganteum*) is the largest living organism on Earth, and is native, primarily, to the Sierra Nevada Mountains of eastern California. The largest sequoia is the General Sherman tree, with a height of 250 feet and a diameter near the base of 24.75 feet. The trunk of the tree weighs almost 1,400 tons.

Released in 2002, the sci-fi comedy *The Adventures of Pluto Nash* is the sixth-largest Hollywood bomb in terms of loss. The movie had a gross budget of $100 million, but earned only $4.41 million at the U.S. box office.

The largest ever jack-o'-lantern was carved from a 1,469-pound pumpkin with a 17-foot circumference by a sculptor in Pennsylvania on Halloween 2005.

The Caterpillar 797B dump truck is currently the largest in the world and has a load capacity of 380 tons. It is powered by a turbocharged diesel engine making 3,550 horsepower. It is 21.5 feet tall, 28 feet wide, and 47.7 feet long, and has an empty operating weight of 278 tons. Each tire is 13 feet tall, weighs four tons, and costs $25,000.

The Cunard cruise ship *Queen Mary 2*, launched in 2003, is the longest, tallest, widest, and heaviest passenger ship ever constructed. The ship measures 1,138.5 feet long, 135.3 feet wide, and 237.6 meters tall, and weighs some 150,000 tons. The ship houses 2,630 passengers and features five swimming pools, 14 restaurants, 24 massage parlors, and an art gallery.

The CargoLifter hangar, located in Brand, Germany, on a former Soviet military airport, is the largest self-supporting hangar in the world. At about 1,200 feet long, 700 feet wide, and 350 feet high, the hangar was designed to accommodate the planned CargoLifter CL 160, an 850-foot-long airship.

Hong Kong has the world's largest double-decker bus fleet in the world.

The biggest hog ever recorded was a creature named Big Boy, who weighed in at 1,904 pounds.

The *Hindenburg* (LZ 129) built by the Zeppelin Company of Germany in 1936 was the largest aircraft ever built and flown. It was 804 feet long, with a maximum diameter of 135 feet, and boasted a 200-foot-long promenade deck. It flew at a top speed of 82 miles per hour, cutting transatlantic travel time by more than two-thirds, and could lift 112 tons beyond its own weight. It was used in transatlantic service for a year before crashing in May 1937.

With faces standing 60 feet tall and 500 feet up, the Mount Rushmore National Monument is the largest art object in the world. The four faces of American presidents George Washington, Thomas Jefferson, Theodore Roosevelt, and Abraham Lincoln are carved into the face of Mount Rushmore in the Black Hills of South Dakota. Sculptor Gutzon Borglum began carving the mountain on August 10, 1927, and, along with 400 workers, worked on the monument until his death in 1941. It was never completed.

The largest cabbage ever grown weighed 144 pounds.

The largest book ever published was *Bhutan: A Visual Odyssey across the Kingdom* by Michael Hawley in 2003. Each book is 5 by 7 feet, 112 pages, and 133 pounds. The book, which costs $2,000 to produce, is sold along with its easel-like stand for $10,000.

The biggest bell is the Tsar Kolokol cast in the Kremlin in 1733. It weighs 216 tons, but was cracked in an accident and never rung.

The largest school in the world is in the Philippines, with an enrollment of about 25,000 students.

The world's largest yo-yo is in the National Yo-Yo Museum in Chico, California. Named Big Yo, the

256-pound yo-yo is an exact scale replica of a Tom Kuhn No Jive 3 in 1 Yo-Yo. Fifty inches tall and 31.5 inches wide, the yo-yo was made in 1979.

Linn's Stamp News is the world's largest weekly newspaper for stamp collectors.

The world's largest weather vane sits on the shores of White Lake in Montague, Michigan. It's 48 feet tall with a 26-foot wind arrow and adorned with a 14-foot replica of a nineteenth-century Great Lakes schooner.

The world's largest coffeepot is located in Davidson, Saskatchewan. It measures 24 feet tall, is made of sheet metal, and can hold 150,000 eight-ounce cups of coffee.

THE BEST OF THE REST

On July 31, 1994, Simon Sang Sung of Singapore turned a single piece of dough into 8,192 noodles in 59.29 seconds—the fastest such a feat was ever completed.

The longest Monopoly game ever played was 1,680 hours long—that's 70 straight days.

The longest-running theater play is the murder mystery *The Mousetrap*, originally called *Three Blind Mice*. It was written by Agatha Christie in 1947 as a 30-minute radio play to celebrate Queen Mary's eightieth birthday. Performance number 20,807 on November 25, 2002, marked its fiftieth anniversary as the world's longest-running play.

The performance was attended by the queen, also celebrating her fiftieth year on the throne. The play has been seen by more than 10 million people and performed in 44 different countries, and it is still running in London.

At the 2004 French Open, Fabrice Santoro and Arnaud Clement played the longest match since the Open era of professional tennis began in 1968. The match began on Monday, May 24, but play was suspended in the fifth set when darkness fell. The game resumed the next day, and Santoro finally beat Clement 16–14 to win the fifth set. The 71-game marathon lasted a total of 6 hours, 33 minutes on court.

The heaviest man recorded was Brower Minnoch of Bainbridge, Oregon, who was admitted to the hospital in Seattle saturated with fluid and suffering from heart and respiratory failure, and weighing more than 1,400 pounds. After 16 months in the hospital, he was discharged at 476 pounds, but was readmitted two years later after regaining almost 200 pounds. When he died in 1983, he weighed more than 798 pounds.

The Mongolian Stock Exchange in Ulaanbaatar, the world's smallest by market capitalization, is housed in a refurbished children's cinema.

The smallest fish in the world is the *Paedocypris progenetica*, a member of the carp family, which is found Indonesia and Sumatra. It grows to 0.31 inches in length.

At seven inches long, the Wilson's storm petrel is the smallest bird to breed on the Antarctic Continent.

The longest snake ever found was a reticulated python, on Sulawesi Island, Indonesia, in 1912. It measured 33 feet. The largest snake ever held in captivity was a python named Colossus, who lived at the Pittsburgh Zoo in Pennsylvania and at the time of her death was 28.5 feet long, had a girth of 37.5 inches, and weighed an estimated 320 pounds.

The cheetah is the fastest mammal on earth and can accelerate from 0 to 45 miles per hour in two seconds. Top speeds of 71 miles an hour can be maintained for up to 300 yards. The fastest cheetahs have been clocked at over 90 miles an hour.

Highest wind velocity ever recorded in the United States was 231 miles per hour, on Mount Washington in New Hampshire, in 1934.

England's Winchester Cathedral has the longest nave in Europe. Writer Jane Austen is buried in the north aisle.

Victor Hugo's *Les Misérables* contains one of the longest sentences in the French language—823 words without a period.

The longest unicycle journey was from Chicago to

Los Angeles. It was made by Steve McPeak in 1968 and took him six weeks.

Shakespeare's most talkative character is Hamlet. None of his other characters has as many lines in a single play, although Falstaff, who appears in several plays, has more lines in total.

China's Great Wall, the world's longest wall, stretches for more than 1,500 miles.

HISTORICALLY ACCURATE

FASHION FORWARD

The Aztec Indians of Mexico believed turquoise would protect them from physical harm, so warriors used these green and blue stones to decorate their battle shields.

More than 5,000 years ago, the Chinese discovered how to make silk from silkworm cocoons. For about 3,000 years, the Chinese kept this discovery a secret.

Because poor people could not afford real silk, they tried to make other cloth look silky. Women would beat on cotton with sticks to soften the fibers. Then they rubbed it against a big stone to make it shiny. The shiny cotton was called "chintz." Because chintz was a cheaper copy of silk, calling something "chintzy" means it is cheap and not of good quality.

The pharaohs of ancient Egypt wore garments made with thin threads of beaten gold. Some fabrics had up to 500 gold threads per one inch of cloth.

The first wooden shoe comes from the Netherlands. The Netherlands has many seas, so people wanted a shoe that kept their feet dry while working outside. The shoes, called *klompen*, were cut from one single piece of wood. Today the *klompen*—or clogs—are the favorite souvenir for people who visit the Netherlands.

During the California gold rush of 1849, miners sent their laundry to Honolulu for washing and pressing. Due to the extremely high costs in California during these boom years, it was deemed more feasible to send the shirts to Hawaii for servicing.

According to the Greek historian Herodotus, Egyptian men never became bald. The reason for this, Herodotus claimed, was that as children Egyptian males had their heads shaved, and their scalps were continually exposed to the health-giving rays of the sun.

False eyelashes were invented by the American film director D. W. Griffith while he was making his 1916 epic *Intolerance*. Griffith wanted actress Seena Owen to have lashes that brushed her cheeks, to make her eyes shine larger than life. A wig maker wove human hair through fine gauze, which was then gummed to Owen's eyelids. *Intolerance* was critically acclaimed but flopped financially, leaving Griffith with huge debts that he might have been able to settle easily . . . had he only thought to patent the eyelashes.

In 1893, Chicago hired its first policewoman, Marie Owens. While the city was progressive in its hiring practices, Chicago's female police officers were not allowed to wear uniforms until 1956.

When wearing a kimono, Japanese women wear socks called *tabi*. The big toe of the sock is separated from the rest of the toes, like a thumb on a mitten.

ANCIENT ER

The ancient Egyptians recommended mixing half an onion with beer foam as a way of warding off death.

The Chinese, in olden days, used marijuana as a remedy for dysentery.

ASSASSINATION ASSOCIATIONS

Abraham Lincoln was elected to Congress in 1846.

John F. Kennedy was elected to Congress in 1946.

Abraham Lincoln was elected President in 1860.

John F. Kennedy was elected President in 1960.

Both were particularly concerned with civil rights.

Both presidents' wives lost children while living in the White House.

Both were shot on a Friday.

Both were shot in the head.

Lincoln's secretary was named Kennedy.

Kennedy's secretary was named Lincoln.

Both were assassinated by Southerners.

Both were succeeded by Southerners named Johnson.

Andrew Johnson, who succeeded Lincoln, was born in 1808.

Lyndon Johnson, who succeeded Kennedy, was born in 1908.

John Wilkes Booth, who assassinated Lincoln, was born in 1839.

Lee Harvey Oswald, who assassinated Kennedy, was born in 1939.

Both assassins were known by their three names. Both names are composed of fifteen letters.

Lincoln was shot at the Ford theater.

Kennedy was shot in a Ford Lincoln car.

Booth ran from the theater and was caught in a warehouse.

Oswald ran from a warehouse and was caught in a theater.

Booth and Oswald were both shot before their trials.

FULLY BOOKED

The first paperback book was printed by Penguin Publishing in 1935.

The first Eskimo Bible was printed in Copenhagen in 1744.

The first dictionary of American English was published on April 14, 1828, by Noah Webster.

The Indian epic poem *The Mahabharata* is eight times longer than *The Iliad* and *The Odyssey* combined.

WORD UP

Scientific America carried the first automobile magazine ad in 1898. The Winton Motor Car Company of Cleveland, Ohio, invited readers to "dispense with a horse."

In 1956, the phrase "In God We Trust" was adopted as the national motto.

Henry Ford flatly stated that history is "bunk."

The last words spoken from the moon were from Eugene Cernan, commander of the *Apollo 17* mission, on December 11, 1972. "As we leave the moon at Taurus-Littrow, we leave as we came, and, God willing, we shall return, with peace and hope for all mankind."

Virginia O'Hanlon Douglas was the eight-year-old girl who, in 1897, asked the staff of the *New York Sun* whether Santa Claus existed. In the now-famous editorial, Francis Church assured Virginia that yes, indeed, "there is a Santa Claus."

John Hancock was the only one of the 50 signatories of the Declaration of Independence who actually signed it on July 4.

On November 29, 1941, the program for the annual Army-Navy football game carried a picture of the battleship *Arizona*, captioned: "It is significant that, despite the claims of air enthusiasts, no battleship has yet been sunk by bombs." Today you can visit the site—now a shrine—where Japanese dive bombers sank the *Arizona* at Pearl Harbor only nine days later.

Leonardo da Vinci could write with one hand and draw with the other simultaneously.

DO NOT PASS GO

Escape maps, compasses, and files were inserted into Monopoly game boards and smuggled into POW camps inside Germany during World War II; real money for escapees was slipped into the packs of Monopoly money.

Values on the Monopoly game board are the same today as they were in 1935.

INVENTOR ADVENTURES

AN UNSURE THING

It has been determined that less than one patented invention in a hundred makes any money for the inventor.

ANCIENT ADVANCEMENTS

The abacus was invented in Egypt in 2000 BC.

Incan soldiers invented the process of freeze-drying food. The process was primitive but effective—potatoes would be left outside to freeze overnight, then thawed and stomped on to remove excess water.

The Greek mathematician Archimedes invented the screw pump. Known as Archimedes' Screw, the device is still used in sewage treatment plants.

The Chinese invented eyeglasses. Marco Polo reported seeing many pairs worn by the Chinese as early as 1275, 500 years before lens grinding became an art in the West.

The ancient Romans invented the arch.

The windmill originated in Iran in AD 644 and was used to grind grain.

BIG BRAINSTORMS

Benjamin Franklin invented swim fins and the rocking chair, among other things.

The first brassiere was invented in 1913 by teenage debutante Mary Phelps Jacob.

Bulletproof vests, fire escapes, windshield wipers, and laser printers were all invented by women.

The parachute was invented 120 years before the airplane. It was intended to save people who had to jump from burning buildings.

When airplanes were still a novel invention, seat belts for pilots were installed only after the consequence of their absence was observed to be fatal—several pilots fell to their deaths while flying upside down.

The first pull-top can was invented by Ermal Cleon Fraze in 1959, after he had to use his car bumper to open a beverage can.

Kleenex tissues were originally invented to remove makeup. Maybe that's why they're still called "facial tissues."

Roulette was invented by Blaise Pascal, a French mathematician and scientist.

In 1916, Jones Wister of Philadelphia invented a rifle for shooting around corners. It had a curved barrel and periscopic sights.

Limelight was how the stage was lit before electricity was invented. Basically, illumination was produced by heating blocks of lime until they glowed.

The same man who led the attack on the Alamo, Mexican military general Antonio Lopez de Santa Anna, is also credited with the invention of chewing gum.

At the turn of the nineteenth century, most light-bulbs were handblown, and one cost the equivalent of half a day's pay for the average worker.

Camel's hair brushes are not made of camel's hair. They were invented by a man named Mr. Camel.

The man who invented shorthand, John Gregg, was deaf.

Because he felt such an important tool should be public

property, English chemist John Walker never patented his invention—matches.

Sylvan N. Goldman of Humpty Dumpty Stores and Standard Food Markets developed the shopping cart so that people could buy more in a single visit to the grocery store. He unveiled his creation in Oklahoma City on June 4, 1937.

In 1832 the Scottish surgeon Neil Arnott devised the waterbed as a way of improving patients' comfort.

American Jim Bristoe invented a 30-foot-long, 2-ton pumpkin cannon that can fire pumpkins up to 5 miles.

FLIGHTS OF FASHION

The modern zipper, the Talon Slide Fastener, was invented in 1913, but didn't catch on until after World War I. The first dresses incorporating the zipper appeared in the 1930s.

The shoestring was invented in England in 1790. Prior to this time, all shoes were fastened with buckles.

Maine was once known as the "earmuff capital of the world," as earmuffs were invented there by Chester Greenwood in 1873.

The safety pin was patented in 1849 by Walter Hunt. He sold the patent rights for $400.

TECH TIMETABLE

Alexander Graham Bell applied for the patent on the telephone three days before he got it to work. Had Bell waited until he had a working model, Elisha Gray, who filed a patent application the same day, would have been awarded the patent. But the telephone system used today is technically more like that described in Gray's patent.

Western Electric invented the loudspeaker, which was initially called a "loud-speaking telephone."

The first commercial vacuum cleaner was so large it was mounted on a wagon. People threw parties in their homes so guests could watch the new device do its job.

The first VCR, made in 1956, was the size of a piano.

In the year 1886, Herman Hollerith had the idea of using punched cards to keep and transport information, a technology used up to the late 1970s. This device was constructed to allow the 1890 census to be tabulated. In 1896, Hollerith founded the Tabulating Machine Company. Twenty-eight years later, in 1924, after several takeovers, the company became known as International Business Machines (IBM).

The first mobile car phones were located in the car's trunk, taking up nearly half of the space.

The City and South London Railway opened the world's first deep-level electric railway on December 18, 1890, from King William Street in the city of London under the River Thames to Stockwell.

Eat, Drink, and Be Merry

HOW SWEET IT IS

It takes one ton of water to make one pound of refined sugar.

A one-kilogram package of sugar will contain about 5 million grains of sugar.

In 1976, the first eight Jelly Belly flavors were launched: Orange, Green Apple, Root Beer, Very Cherry, Lemon, Cream Soda, Grape, and Licorice.

A honeybee must tap 2 million flowers to make one pound of honey. A bee produces only one-twelfth of a teaspoon of honey during her entire lifetime.

The world's first chocolate sweet was produced in 1828 by Dutch chocolate-maker Conrad J. Van Houten. He pressed the fat from roasted cacao beans to produce cocoa butter, to which he added cocoa powder and sugar.

Americans consumed more than 3.1 billion pounds of chocolate in 2001, which is almost half of the total world's production.

A 1.5-ounce milk chocolate bar has only 220 calories.

A recent study indicates that, when men crave food, they tend to crave fat and salt. When women crave food, they tend to desire chocolate.

American and Russian space flights have always included chocolate.

The bestselling chocolate bar in Russia is Snickers.

Per capita, the Irish eat more chocolate than Americans, Swedes, Danes, French, and Italians.

American chocolate manufacturers use about 1.5 billion pounds of milk, which is only surpassed by the cheese and ice cream industries.

Aztec emperor Montezuma drank 50 golden goblets of hot chocolate every day. It was thick, dyed red, and flavored with chili peppers.

Hostess Twinkies were invented in 1931 by James Dewar, manager of Continental Bakeries' Chicago factory. He envisioned the product as a way of using the company's thousands of shortcake pans, which were otherwise employed only during the strawberry season. Originally called Little Shortcake Fingers, they were renamed Twinkie Fingers, and finally Twinkies.

More than 180 million Cadbury's Creme Eggs are sold between January and Easter each year.

Nabisco's Oreo is the world's bestselling brand of cookie, at a rate of 6 billion each year. The first Oreo was sold in 1912.

The daughter of confectioner Leo Hirschfield is commemorated in the name of the sweet he invented. Although his daughter's real name was Clara, she went by the nickname Tootsie and, in her honor, her doting father named his chewy chocolate logs Tootsie Rolls.

The first ring doughnuts were produced in 1847 by a 15-year-old baker's apprentice, Hanson Gregory, who knocked the soggy center out of a fried doughnut.

Laws forbidding the sale of sodas on Sunday prompted William Garwood to invent the ice cream sundae in Evanston in 1875.

The ice cream soda was invented in 1874 by Robert Green. He was serving a mixture of syrup, sweet cream, and carbonated water at a celebration in Philadelphia. He ran out of cream and substituted ice cream.

A black cow is a chocolate soda with chocolate ice cream.

Chocolate chip cookies are the baked goods most likely to cause tooth decay. Pies, un-iced cakes, and doughnuts are less harmful to the teeth.

It takes as much as 50 gallons of maple sap to make a single gallon of maple sugar.

Vanilla is the extract of fermented and dried pods of several species of orchids.

Thirty-five million pounds of candy corn is produced every year in America, which is enough to circle the moon four times.

RABBIT FOOD

The carrot belongs to the family *Umbelliferae*. The wild variety is classified as *Daucus carota*; both of the words in *Daucus carota* mean orange.

The carrot is a member of the parsley family, including species such as celery, parsnip, fennel, dill, and coriander.

The ancient Greeks called carrots *karoto*.

The Japanese word for carrot is *ninjin*.

Carrots produce more distilled spirit than potatoes.

Carrot flowers are also called birds' nest, bees' nest, and the devil's plague.

The classic Bugs Bunny carrot is the Danvers type.

Holtville, California, dubs itself the "carrot capital of the world" and has an annual festival.

Carrot oil is used for flavoring and in perfumery. An extract of carrots was used to color oleo (margarine) during the fats rationing that took place during World War II.

The Greek foot soldiers who hid in the Trojan Horse were said to have consumed ample quantities of raw carrots to deactivate their bowels.

In early Celtic literature, the carrot is referred to as the "honey underground."

It is alleged that Nero ate the last remaining root of the ancient carrot sylphion.

Tobacconists in France used to put a carrot in their bins to keep their tobacco from drying out.

The Greeks thought that carrots cured venereal disease. Arab cultures thought they were a possible aphrodisiac.

In Scotland, the Sunday before Michaelmas, September 29, is called Carrot Sunday.

Americans know the wild carrot as Queen Anne's lace, rattlesnake weed, and American carrot.

A Cleveland man has a collection of more than 10,000 carrot items.

The longest carrot recorded in 1996 was 16 feet, 10.5 inches. The heaviest carrot recorded in the world, in 1998, was a single root mass weighing 18.985 pounds.

There is a carrot-pie flavor jelly bean.

Carrots have the highest vitamin A content of all vegetables.

Carrots are not always orange and can also be found in purple, white, red, or yellow.

Carrots were first grown as a medicine, not a food.

In Suffolk, carrots were formerly given as a remedy for preserving and restoring the wind of horses.

Eleven pounds of carrots contain 1 ounce and 11 grains of sugar.

The Anglo-Saxons included carrots as an ingredient in a medicinal drink against the devil and insanity.

Most common food plants contain natural poisons. Carrots, for example, contain carotatoxin, myristicin, isoflavones, and nitrates.

🥜 BANANA REPUBLIC

Some horticulturists suspect that the banana was the Earth's first fruit. Banana plants have been in cultivation since the time of recorded history. One of the first records of bananas dates back to Alexander the Great's conquest of India, where he discovered bananas in 327 BC.

Banana plants are the largest plants on Earth without a woody stem. They are actually giant herbs of the same family as lilies, orchids, and palms.

Bananas are perennial crops that are grown and harvested year round. The banana plant does not grow from a seed, but rather from a rhizome or bulb. Each fleshy bulb pound will sprout new shoots year after year.

As bananas ripen, the starch in the fruit turns to sugar. Therefore, the riper the banana, the sweeter it will taste.

A cluster of bananas is called a hand and consists of 10 to 20 bananas, which are known as fingers. The word *banan* is Arabic for finger.

Bananas are one of the few fruits that ripen best off the plant. If left on the plant, the fruit splits open and the pulp has a "cottony" texture and flavor. Even in tropical growing areas, bananas for domestic consumption are cut green and stored in moist shady places to ripen slowly.

In 1516, Friar Tomas sailed to the Caribbean from Europe bringing banana roots with him; he planted bananas in the rich fertile soil of the tropics, thus beginning the banana's future in American life. Bananas were officially introduced to the American public at the 1876 Philadelphia Centennial Exhibition. The banana is now the most widely eaten fruit in America.

Bananas have no fat, cholesterol, or sodium.

In eastern Africa a popular item is banana beer, brewed from bananas.

In Southeast Asia the banana leaf is used to wrap food, providing a unique flavor and aroma to *nasi lemak* and Indian banana leaf rice.

India is by far the largest world producer of bananas, growing 16.5 million tons in 2002, followed by Brazil, which produced 6.5 million tons of bananas in 2002. To the Indians, the flower from the banana tree is sacred. During religious and important ceremonies such as weddings, banana flowers are tied around the head, as they believe this will bring good luck.

VEGETABLE MEDLEY

The term "vegetable" is not a botanical term; therefore just about any part of a plant can be considered a vegetable.

The tomato is commonly considered a vegetable even though botanically it is a fruit. The U.S. Supreme Court unanimously ruled that the tomato was a vegetable for the purposes of the 1883 Tariff Act based on a definition that classifies vegetables by use. It is the state vegetable of New Jersey, but both the state fruit and the state vegetable of Arkansas. Other vegetables that are botanically considered fruit include egg-plants, cucumbers, and squashes.

Americans eat more than 22 pounds of tomatoes every year. More than half this amount is eaten in the form of ketchup and tomato sauce.

Most store-bought pumpkins in the United States were originally grown in Illinois, California, Ohio, or Pennsylvania, which produced more than 9 million pounds of pumpkins combined in 2005.

The number of seeds in a pumpkin can be accurately de-termined, give or take 10 seeds, by multiplying the num-ber of fruiting sections by 16.

Two-thirds of the world's eggplant is grown in New Jersey.

Spinach is native to Iran and didn't spread to other parts of the world until the beginning of the Christian era.

Ancient Greeks and Romans believed asparagus had medicinal qualities for helping to prevent bee stings and relieve toothaches.

Research shows that only 43 percent of homemade din-ners served in the United States include vegetables. How-ever, Americans eat 18 percent more vegetables today than they did in 1970.

FRUITY FACTS

Lemons have more sugar than oranges.

Ninety-five percent of the entire lemon crop produced in the United States is from California and Arizona.

Thin-skinned lemons are the juiciest.

There are more than 7,000 varieties of apples grown in the world. China produces more apples than the rest of the world put together. The apples from one tree can fill 20 boxes every year. Each box weighs an average of 42 pounds.

Americans eat an average of 18 pounds of fresh apples each year. The most popular variety in the United States is the red delicious.

The difference between apple juice and apple cider is that the juice is pasteurized and the cider is not.

Grapes explode when put in the microwave.

The Agen plum, which became the basis of the U.S. prune industry, was first planted in California in 1856.

More than 1,200 varieties of watermelon are grown in 96 countries worldwide. There are about 200 varieties of watermelon throughout the United States. Cousin to the cucumber and kin to the gourd, watermelons can range in size from 7 to 100 pounds.

In 2005 the Bright family from Arkansas grew the world's largest watermelon, weighing in at 268.8 pounds.

Olives, which grow on trees, were first cultivated 5,000 years ago in Syria.

TASTY INVENTIONS

California's Frank Epperson invented the Popsicle in 1905 when he was 11 years old.

Aunt Jemima Pancake Flour, invented in 1889, was the first ready-mix food to be sold commercially.

Fortune cookies were invented in 1916 by George Jung, a Los Angeles noodle maker.

Caesar salad has nothing to do with any of the historical Caesars. It was first concocted in a restaurant in Tijuana, Mexico, in the 1920s, by a man named Caesar Cardini.

To make haggis, the national dish of Scotland, take the heart, liver, lungs, and small intestine of a calf or sheep, boil them in the stomach of the animal, season with salt, pepper, and onions, and add suet and oatmeal.

In 1926, when a Los Angeles restaurant owner with the all-American name of Bob Cobb was looking for a way to use up leftovers, he threw together some avocado, celery, tomato, chives, watercress, hard-boiled eggs, chicken, bacon, and Roquefort cheese, and named it after himself: a Cobb salad.

Goulash, a beef soup, originated in Hungary in the ninth century.

Buttered bread was invented by the astronomer Copernicus. He was trying to find a cure for the plague.

Mayonnaise is said to be the invention of the French chef of the Duke de Richelieu in 1756. While the duke was defeating the British at Port Mahon, his chef was creating a victory feast that included a sauce made of cream and eggs. When the chef realized that there was no cream in the kitchen, he improvised, substituting olive oil for the cream. A new culinary masterpiece was born, and the chef named it *Mahonnaise* in honor of the duke's victory.

Sliced bread was introduced under the Wonder Bread label in 1930.

Swiss steak, chop suey, and Russian dressing all originated in the United States.

The hamburger was invented in 1900 by Louis Lassen at his sandwich shop in New Haven, Connecticut. He ground beef, broiled it, and served it between two pieces of toast.

The city of Denver claims to have invented the cheeseburger.

Potato chips were invented in Saratoga Springs in 1853 by chef George Crum. They were a mocking response to a patron who complained that his french fries were too thick.

Popcorn was invented by the American Indians.

Potatoes, pineapples, and pumpkins originate from Peru.

The original recipe for margarine was milk, lard, and sheep's stomach lining.

HYDRATION HAPPENINGS

In a Washington study, one glass of water stopped midnight hunger pangs for almost 100 percent of the dieters studied.

Lack of water is the main trigger of daytime fatigue. A mere 2 percent drop in body water can trigger fuzzy short-term memory, trouble with basic math, and difficulty focusing on the computer screen or on a printed page.

Even mild dehydration will slow down one's metabolism by as much as 3 percent.

It takes almost nine calories—the equivalent of eating one gummy bear—for the body to warm up eight ounces of 32-degree ice water after drinking it.

Preliminary research indicates that eight to ten glasses of water a day could significantly ease back and joint pain for up to 80 percent of sufferers.

Water is the official state beverage of Indiana.

🌰 TEA-TOTALERS

A common drink for Tibetans is butter tea, which is made out of butter, salt, and brick tea.

When tea was first introduced in the American colonies, many housewives, in their ignorance, served the tea leaves with sugar or syrup after throwing away the water in which they had been boiled.

There are professional tea tasters as well as wine tasters.

GOT MILK?

Humans are the only species who drink milk from the mothers of other species.

Camel's milk doesn't curdle.

Goat milk is used to produce Roquefort cheese.

Sixty cows can produce a ton of milk a day.

Soymilk, the liquid left after beans have been crushed in hot water and strained, is a favorite beverage in the East.

In Hong Kong, soymilk is as popular as Coca-Cola is in the United States.

🌰 CHEESED OFF

The Uruguayan army once won a sea battle using Edam cheeses as cannonballs.

In 1987, a 1,400-year-old lump of still edible cheese was unearthed in Ireland.

When Swiss cheese ferments, a bacterial action generates gas. As the gas is liberated, it bubbles through the cheese leaving holes. Cheese makers call them "eyes."

YOU SAY POTATO, I SAY . . .

The white potato originated in the Andes Mountains and was probably brought to Britain by Sir Francis Drake about 1586.

When potatoes first appeared in Europe in the seventeenth century, it was thought that they were disgusting, and they were blamed for starting outbreaks of leprosy and syphilis. As late as 1720 in America, eating potatoes was believed to shorten a person's life.

During the Alaskan Klondike gold rush, potatoes were so valued for their vitamin C content that miners traded gold for potatoes.

In the United States, one pound of potato chips costs 200 times more than one pound of potatoes. Potato chips are American's favorite snack food. They are devoured at a rate of 1.2 billion pounds a year.

Britons eat more than 22,000 tons of french fries a week.

McDonald's and Burger King sugarcoat their fries so they will turn golden-brown.

TO EVERYTHING THERE IS A SEASONING

Black pepper is the most popular spice in the world.

Saffron, made from the dried stamens of cultivated crocus flowers, is the most expensive cooking spice.

Capsaicin, which makes peppers "hot" to the human mouth, is best neutralized by casein, the main protein found in milk.

The hottest chili in the world is the habanero.

The color of a chili is no indication of its spiciness, but size usually is—the smaller the pepper, the hotter it is.

Although the combination of chili peppers and oregano for seasoning has been traced to the ancient Aztecs, the present blend is said to be the invention of early Texans. Chili powder today is typically a blend of dried chilies, garlic powder, red peppers, oregano, and cumin.

Table salt is the only commodity that hasn't risen dramatically in price in the last 150 years.

GREAT GRAINS

Rice is the staple food of more than one-half of the world's population.

There are more than 15,000 different kinds of rice.

Rice needs more water to grow than any other crop.

During World War II, bakers in the United States were ordered to stop selling sliced bread for the duration of the war on January 18, 1943. Only whole loaves were made available to the public. It was never explained how this action helped the war effort.

In 1983, a Japanese artist made a copy of the *Mona Lisa* completely out of toast.

There are more than 225 different kinds of bread in Germany.

A 1991 Gallup survey indicated that 49 percent of Americans didn't know that white bread is made from wheat.

The wheat that produces a one-pound loaf of bread requires two tons of water to grow.

On average, a baby in the United States will eat 15 pounds of cereal in the first year of life.

MEATY TOPICS

Americans consumed more than 20 billion hot dogs in 2000.

When American children were asked what they would like on their hot dogs if their mothers weren't watching, 25 percent said they would prefer chocolate sauce.

Goat meat contains up to 45 percent less saturated fat than chicken meat.

"Colonial goose" is the name Australians give to stuffed mutton.

The dye used to stamp the grade on meat is edible and is made from grape skins.

Pigturducken is a pig, stuffed with a turkey, which is stuffed with a duck, stuffed with a chicken, deep fried in oil.

The largest item on any menu in the world is probably the roast camel, sometimes served at Bedouin wedding feasts. The camel is stuffed with a sheep's carcass, which is stuffed with chickens, which are stuffed with fish, which are stuffed with eggs.

A typical American eats 28 pigs in a lifetime.

Worldwide consumption of pork exceeds that of any other type of meat.

It is illegal to import pork products into Yemen, with a maximum punishment of death.

People in Sweden eat about one kilogram of ham per person each Christmas.

A single sausage measuring 5,917 feet in length was cooked in Barcelona, Spain, on September 22, 1986.

PASSION FOR POULTRY

China's Beijing Duck Restaurant can seat 9,000 people at one time.

Fried chicken is the most popular meal ordered in sit-down restaurants in the United States. The next in popularity are roast beef, spaghetti, turkey, baked ham, and fried shrimp.

In 1995, Kentucky Fried Chicken sold 11 pieces of chicken for every man, woman, and child in the United States.

In an authentic Chinese meal, the last course is soup because it allows the roast duck entree to "swim" toward digestion.

Persians first began using colored eggs to celebrate spring in 3000 BC, and thirteenth-century Macedonians were the first Christians on record to use colored eggs in Easter celebrations. Crusaders returning from the Middle East spread the custom of coloring eggs, and Europeans began to use them to celebrate Easter and other warm-weather holidays.

A hard-boiled egg will spin. An uncooked or soft-boiled egg will not. An egg that is fresh will sink in water, but a stale one won't.

The white part of an egg is called the albumen.

Washing a chicken egg will strip it of natural coatings that keep out bacteria; it will rot very quickly thereafter.

A turkey should never be carved until it has been out of the oven at least 30 minutes. This permits the inner cooking to subside and the internal meat juices to stop running. Once the meat sets, it's easier to carve clean, neat slices.

Native Americans never actually ate turkey; killing such a timid bird was thought to indicate laziness.

The dark meat on a roast turkey has more calories than the white meat.

GOING NUTS

Most nuts will remain fresh for a year, if kept in their shells.

Macadamia nuts are not sold in their shells because it takes 300 pounds per square inch of pressure to break the shell.

It takes more than 500 peanuts to make one 12-ounce jar of peanut butter. The FDA allows an average of 30 or more insect fragments and one or more rodent hairs per 100 grams of peanut butter.

FOOD HANDLERS

During the Middle Ages, almost all beef, pork, mutton, and chicken were chopped finely. Forks were unknown at the time, and the knife was a kitchen utensil rather than a piece of tableware.

When Catherine de Medici married Henry II of France in 1533, she brought forks with her as well as several master Florentine cooks. Foods never before seen in France were soon being served using utensils instead of fingers or daggers. She is said to have introduced spinach, used in dishes "à la Florentine," as well as aspics, sweetbreads, artichoke hearts, truffles, liver *crépinettes*, quenelles of poultry, macaroons, ice cream, and zabagliones.

The Chinese developed the custom of using chopsticks

because they didn't need anything resembling a knife and fork at the table. They cut up food into bite sized pieces in the kitchen before serving it. This stemmed from their belief that bringing meat to the table in any form resembling an animal was uncivilized, and that it was also inhospitable to ask a guest to cut food while eating.

FUNGI SIDE

The fungus called truffles can cost $225 to $425 per pound. They are sniffed out by female pigs, which detect a compound that is also in the saliva of male pigs. The same chemical is found in the sweat of human males.

Mushrooms have no chlorophyll so they don't need sunshine to grow and thrive. Some of the earliest commercial mushroom farms were set up in caves in France during the reign of King Louis XIV.

The largest living organism ever found is a honey mushroom (*Armillaria ostoyae*). It covers 3.4 square miles of land in the Blue Mountains of eastern Oregon, and is still growing.

The world's deadliest mushroom is the *Amanita phalloides*, the death cap. The five different poisons contained by the mushroom cause diarrhea and vomiting within six to twelve hours of ingestion. This is followed by damage to the liver, kidneys, and central nervous system—and, in the majority of cases, coma and death.

BUG JUICE

In South Africa, termites are often roasted and eaten by the handful, like pretzels or popcorn.

According to many who've tried them, beetles taste like apples, wasps like pine nuts, and worms like fried bacon.

A pound of houseflies contains more protein than a pound of beef.

EPICURIOUS

The first product with a bar code to be scanned at a checkout was a pack of Wrigley's Juicy Fruit chewing gum.

Chewing gum while cutting onions can help prevent tearing up.

Refried beans aren't really what they seem. Although their name seems like a reasonable translation of Spanish *frijoles refritos*, the fact is that these beans aren't fried twice. In Spanish, *refritos* literally means "well-fried," not "refried."

The English word "soup" comes from the Middle Ages word "sop," which means a slice of bread over which roast drippings were poured. The first archaeological evidence of soup being consumed dates back to 6000 BC, with the main ingredient being hippopotamus bones.

The herring is the most widely eaten fish in the world. Nutritionally, its fuel value is equal to that of a beefsteak.

The ancient Greeks thought that eating cabbage would cure a hangover, and the ancient Romans thought that eating fried canaries would do the same.

Van Camp's Pork and Beans were a staple food for Union soldiers in the Civil War.

The Chinese used to open shrimp by flaying the shells with bamboo poles. Until recently, in factories where dried shrimp were being prepared, "shrimp dancers" were hired to tramp on the shells with special shoes.

There are 2 million different combinations of sandwiches that can be created from a Subway menu.

During Thanksgiving and the Super Bowl, food consumption is larger than any other day in the United States.

Coffee Klatch

BREW BASICS

Coffee is the most popular beverage worldwide with more than 400 billion cups consumed each year. Coffee is grown commercially in more than 45 countries throughout the world—all of which lie along the equator between the Tropics of Cancer and Capricorn.

Coffee, along with beer and peanut butter, is on a list of the "ten most recognizable odors." As a world commodity, it is second only to oil.

In 1727, using seedlings smuggled from Paris, coffee plants were first cultivated in Brazil. Brazil is now by far the world's largest producer of coffee, accounting for almost one-third of the world's coffee production and producing more than 3.33 billion pounds of coffee each year. More than 5 million people in Brazil are employed by the coffee trade.

The most widely accepted legend associated with the discovery of coffee is of the goat herder named Kaldi of Ethiopia. Around the year AD 800–850, Kaldi was amazed as he noticed his goats behaving in a frisky manner after eating the leaves and berries of a coffee shrub, and decided he had to try them himself.

The Arabs are generally believed to have been the first to brew coffee. The first commercially grown and harvested coffee originated in the Arabian Peninsula near the port of Mocha. Turkey began to roast and grind the coffee bean in the thirteenth century and, by the sixteenth century the country had become the chief distributor of coffee, with markets established in Egypt, Syria, Persia, and Venice. Coffee was first known in Europe as Arabian wine.

In the sixteenth century, Turkish women could divorce their husbands if the man failed to keep his family's pot filled with coffee.

Beethoven was a coffee lover, and so particular about his coffee that he always counted 60 beans for each cup when he prepared his brew.

French philosopher Voltaire reportedly drank 50 cups of coffee a day.

The first coffee mill appeared in London during the seventeenth century.

Coffee as a medicine reached its highest and lowest point in the seventeenth century in England. Wild medical contraptions to administer a mixture of coffee and an assortment of heated butter, honey, and oil became treatments for the sick. Advertisements for coffee in London in 1657 claimed that the beverage was a cure for scurvy, gout, and other ills.

The first Parisian café opened in 1689 to serve coffee. Before the rise of coffeehouses, coffee was sold by street vendors in Europe in the Arab fashion, the forerunners of the pavement espresso carts of today.

In 1763 there were more than 200 coffee shops in Venice. Italy now has more than 200,000 coffee bars.

Until the eighteenth century, coffee was almost always boiled.

The drip pot was invented by a Frenchman around 1800.

By 1850 the manual coffee grinder had found its way to most upper-middle-class kitchens of the Western world.

The first commercial espresso machine was manufactured in Italy in 1906.

The coffee filter was invented in 1908 by Melitta Benz, a German homemaker, when she lined a tin cup with blotter paper to filter the coffee grinds.

In Italy, espresso is considered so essential to daily life that if it is consumed at the bar, the price is regulated by the government. Italians do not usually drink espresso during meals.

The average age of an Italian *barista* is 48 years old. A *barista* is a respected job title in Italy.

Australians consume 60 percent more coffee than tea, a sixfold increase since 1940.

In Japan, coffee shops are called *kissaten*. More than 10,000 coffee shops plus several thousand vending machines with both hot and cold coffee serve the needs of Tokyo alone. The official Coffee Day in Japan is October 1. Japan ranks third in the world in coffee consumption.

Scandinavia has the world's highest per capita annual coffee consumption, 26.4 pounds. Italy has an annual consumption per capita of only 10 pounds.

In Sumatra, workers on coffee plantations gather the world's most expensive coffee by following a gourmet marsupial who consumes only the choicest coffee beans. By picking through what he excretes, they obtain the world's most expensive coffee—Kopi Luwak, which sells for more than $100 per pound.

Raw coffee beans, soaked in water and spices, are chewed like sweets in many parts of Africa.

THE NATIONAL DRINK

Coffee represents 75 percent of all the caffeine consumed in the United States. Fifty-two percent of Americans drink coffee. The United States is the world's largest consumer of coffee, importing 16 to 20 million bags annually (2.5 million pounds), representing one-third of all coffee exported. The typical coffee drinker has 3.4 cups of coffee per day. That translates into more than 450 million cups of coffee daily. The average annual coffee consumption of an American adult is 26.7 gallons, or more than 400 cups.

In 1670, Dorothy Jones of Boston was granted a license to sell coffee, and so became the first American coffee trader.

William Penn purchased a pound of coffee in New York in 1683 for $4.68.

The heavy tea tax imposed on the colonies in 1773, which led to the Boston Tea Party, resulted in America switching from tea to coffee.

In 1790 there were two coffee firsts in the United States: the first wholesale coffee roasting company, and the first newspaper advertisement featuring coffee.

During the Civil War, Union soldiers were issued 8 pounds of ground roasted coffee as part of their personal ration of 100 pounds of food.

In the early 1900s, coffee was often delivered door-to-door in the United States, by horse-pulled wagons.

During World War II, the government used 260 million pounds of instant coffee.

In 1990, more than 4 billion dollars' worth of coffee was imported into the United States.

The largest coffee import center in the United States is located in the city of New Orleans.

Hawaii features an annual Kona Festival, a coffee-picking contest. Each year the winner becomes a state celebrity. Hawaii is the only state of the United States in which coffee is commercially grown, and the coffee is harvested between November and April.

FEELING CAFFEINATED

There are about 30 milligrams of caffeine in the average chocolate bar, while a cup of coffee contains around 100 to 150.

Caffeine is on the International Olympic Committee list of prohibited substances. Athletes who test positive for more than 12 micrograms of caffeine per milliliter of urine may be banned from the Olympic Games. This level may be reached after drinking about five cups of coffee.

Special studies conducted about the human body reveal it will usually absorb up to about 300 milligrams of caffeine at a given time—about four normal cups. Additional amounts are just cast off, providing no further stimulation. The human body dissipates 20 percent of the caffeine in the system each hour.

Espresso vendors report an increase in decaffeinated sales in the month of January due to New Year's resolutions to decrease caffeine intake.

🐚 A HEALTHY HABIT?

A scientific report from the University of California found that the steam rising from a cup of coffee contains the same amounts of antioxidants as three oranges. The antioxidants are heterocyclic compounds that prevent cancer and heart disease.

Regular coffee drinkers have about one-third less asthma symptoms than non–coffee drinkers do, according to a Harvard researcher who studied 20,000 people.

Large doses of coffee can be lethal. Ten grams, or 100 cups over four hours, can kill the average human.

THE DAILY GRIND

Coffee is graded according to three criteria: bean quality (altitude and species), quality of preparation, and size of bean.

When a coffee seed is planted, it takes about five years to yield consumable fruit.

Coffee trees are self-pollinating.

The arabica is the original coffee plant, which still grows wild in Ethiopia. The arabica coffee tree is an evergreen, and in the wild will grow to a height between 14 and 20 feet. Coffee trees are normally pruned to around 8 feet in order to facilitate harvesting.

Coffee trees produce highly aromatic, short-lived flowers generating a scent between jasmine and orange. These blossoms produce cranberry-size coffee cherries. It takes four to five years to yield a commercial harvest. Thereafter, the tree produces consistently for 15 or 20 years.

An acre of coffee trees can produce up to 10,000 pounds of coffee cherries. That amounts to approximately 2,000 pounds of beans after hulling or milling. An arabica coffee tree can produce up to 12 pounds of coffee a year, depending on soil and climate.

The 2,000 arabica coffee cherries it takes to make a roasted pound of coffee are normally picked by hand as they ripen. Since each cherry contains two beans, it takes about 4,000 arabica beans to make a pound of roasted coffee.

Only about 20 percent of harvested coffee beans are considered to be a premium bean of the highest quality.

Coffee sacks are usually made of hemp and weigh approximately 132 pounds when they are full of green coffee beans. It takes more than 600,000 beans to fill a coffee sack.

Coffee beans are similar to grapes that produce wine in that they are affected by the temperature, soil conditions, altitude, rainfall, drainage, and degree of ripeness when picked.

After decaffeinating coffee, processing companies no longer throw the caffeine away; they sell it to pharmaceutical companies.

Before roasting, some green coffee beans are stored for years, and experts believe that certain beans improve with age when stored properly.

Until the late nineteenth century, people roasted their coffee at home using popcorn poppers and stove-top frying pans.

Coffee is generally roasted between 400°F and 425°F. The longer it is roasted, the darker the roast. Roasting time is usually 10 to 20 minutes. Dark-roasted coffees actually have less caffeine than medium roasts. The longer a coffee is roasted, the more caffeine burns off during the process.

Overroasted coffee beans are very flammable during the roasting process.

After coffee beans are roasted, and when they begin to cool, they release about 700 chemical substances that make up the vaporizing aromas.

FLAVOR PROFILES

The aroma and flavor derived from coffee is a result of the little beads of the oily substance called coffee essence, or coffee oil. This is not actual oil since it dissolves in water.

Roasted coffee beans start to lose small amounts of flavor within two weeks. Ground coffee begins to lose its flavor in one hour. Brewed coffee and espresso begins to lose flavor within minutes.

Finely grinding coffee beans and boiling them in water is still known as "Turkish coffee." It is still made this way today in Turkey and Greece. An old Turkish proverb says, "Coffee should be black as hell, strong as death, and as sweet as love."

Commercially flavored coffee beans are flavored with special oils after they are roasted and partially cooled to around 100 degrees, when the coffee beans' pores are open and therefore more receptive to flavor absorption.

Irish cream and hazelnut are the most popular whole bean coffee flavorings.

Frederick the Great had his coffee made with champagne and a bit of mustard.

Milk as an additive to coffee became popular in the 1680s, when a French physician recommended that café au lait be used for medicinal purposes.

Adding sugar to coffee is believed to have started in 1715, in the court of Louis XIV.

Iced coffee in a can has been popular in Japan since 1945.

The Europeans first added chocolate to their coffee in the seventeenth century.

Citrus has been added to coffee for several hundred years.

Dandelion root can be roasted and ground as a coffee substitute.

To make espresso sweet, use granulated sugar, which dissolves more quickly, rather than sugar cubes; white sugar rather than brown sugar; and real sugar rather than sweeteners, which alter the taste of coffee.

Jamaican Blue Mountain coffee is one of the most expensive and sought-after coffees in the world.

The word "cappuccino" has several derivations, the original of which began in the sixteenth century. The Capuchin order of friars, established after 1525, played an important role in bringing Catholicism back to Reformation Europe. Its Italian name came from the long pointed cowl, or *cappuccino*, "hood," that was worn as part of the order's habit. The French version of *cappuccino* was *capuchin*, from which came the English Capuchin. In Italian, cappuccino went on to describe espresso coffee mixed or topped with steamed milk or cream, so called because the color of the coffee resembled the color of the habit of a Capuchin friar. The first use of cappuccino in English is recorded in 1948 in a work about San Francisco. There is also the story that says that the term comes from the fact that the coffee is dark, like the monk's robe, and the cap is likened to the color of the monk's head.

Spirited Away

ALL ABOUT ALCOHOL

Alcohol is derived from the Arabic *al kohl*, meaning "the essence."

Alcohol beverages have been produced for at least 12,000 years. The consumption of alcohol was so widespread throughout history that it has been called "a universal language."

To determine the percentage of alcohol in a bottle of liquor, divide the proof by two.

The strongest that any alcohol beverage can be is 190 proof (or 95 percent alcohol). At a higher proof, the beverage draws moisture from the air and self-dilutes.

The alcohol in drinks of either low alcohol content (below 15 percent) or high alcohol content (over 30 percent) tend to be absorbed into the body more slowly.

It's impossible to create a beverage of more than 18 percent alcohol by fermentation alone.

Methyphobia is fear of alcohol.

Most vegetable and virtually all fruit juices contain alcohol.

Temperance activists, who strongly opposed the consumption of alcohol, typically consumed patent medicines that, just like whiskey, generally contained 40 percent alcohol.

Some studies suggest that drinking alcohol in moderation reduces the risk of heart disease by an average of about 40 percent.

Research evidence from around the world generally shows that countries with higher alcohol consumption have fewer drinking problems than those countries where consumption is relatively low.

Studying the experimentally induced intoxicated behavior of ants in 1888, naturalist John Lubbock noticed that insects that had too much to drink were picked up by nest mates and carried home. Conversely, drunken stranger ants were summarily tossed in a ditch.

Contrary to a common misconception, alcohol does not

destroy brain cells. In fact, the moderate consumption of alcohol is often associated with improved cognitive functioning. One can limit the effect of alcohol by eating and by not consuming more than one drink per hour. High-protein foods such as cheese and peanuts help slow the absorption of alcohol into the body.

All 13 minerals necessary for human life can be found in alcohol beverages.

Alcohol consumption decreases during the time of the full moon.

Drinking alcohol lowers rather than raises the body's temperature.

There is a cloud of alcohol in outer space with enough alcohol to make 4 trillion trillion drinks. It's free for the taking—but it's 10,000 light-years away from Earth.

Regardless of sex, age, or weight, it takes one hour for .015 percent of blood alcohol content to leave the body. It takes 10 hours for a person with a blood alcohol content of 0.15 percent to become completely sober. Giving a drunk person coffee will merely produce a wide-awake drunk.

Every person produces alcohol normally in the body 24 hours each and every day from birth until death.

A Chinese imperial edict of about 1116 BC asserted

that the use of alcohol in moderation was required by heaven.

To the pre-Christian Anglo-Saxons, heaven was not a place to play harps, but a place to visit with other departed souls and enjoy alcohol beverages.

The word "symposium" originally referred to a gathering of men in ancient Greece for an evening of conversation and drinking.

According to the Gospels, Jesus drank alcohol (Matthew 15:11; Luke 7:33–35) and approved of its moderate consumption (Matthew 15:11). Saint Paul considered alcohol to be a creation of God and inherently good (1 Timothy 4:4). The early Church declared that alcohol was an inherently good gift of God to be used and enjoyed. While individuals might choose not to drink, to despise alcohol was heresy.

During the Middle Ages it was mainly the monasteries that maintained the knowledge and skills necessary to produce good-quality alcohol beverages.

Distillation was developed during the Middle Ages, and the resulting alcohol was called aqua vitae or "water of life."

The adulteration of alcohol beverages was punishable by death in medieval Scotland.

Drinking liqueurs was required at all treaty signings during the Middle Ages.

An 18-year study by the National Institute on Aging found that men age 50 and older who consumed a drink a day during middle age scored significantly better on cognitive tests later in life than nondrinkers did.

Each molecule of alcohol is less than a billionth of a meter long and consists of a few atoms of oxygen, carbon, and hydrogen.

The alcohol content of the typical bottle of beer, glass of wine, and mixed drink are equivalent.

One glass of milk can give a person a .02 blood alcohol concentration on a Breathalyzer test, enough in some states for persons under the legal drinking age to lose their driver's license or be fined.

Fermentation within the body is essential for human life to exist. Fermentation is involved in the production of many foods, including bread (bread "rises" as it ferments), sauerkraut, coffee, black tea, cheese, yogurt, buttermilk, pickles, cottage cheese, chocolate, vanilla, ginger, ketchup, mustard, soy sauce, and many more.

BEERFEST

There are 27 different styles of beer, and 49 substyles.

Germany produces more than 5,000 varieties of beer and has about 1,300 breweries.

Beck's is not only Germany's top export beer, it also accounts for 85 percent of all German beer exports to the United States.

There are 19 different versions of Guinness.

The bubbles in Guinness beer sink to the bottom rather than float to the top as in other beers.

In Welsh, the word for beer is *cwrw*, pronounced "koo-roo."

According to a journal entry from 1636, farm workers in the colony of Quebec not only received an allowance of flour, lard, oil, vinegar, and codfish, but were also given "a chopine of cider a day or a quart of beer."

For beer commercials, liquid detergent is added to the beer to make it foam more.

Bottle caps, or "crowns," were invented in Baltimore in 1892 by William Painter. Painter proved his invention's worth when he convinced a local brewer to ship a few hundred cases of beer to South America and back, and they returned without a leak.

Unlike wines, most beers should be stored upright to minimize oxidation and metal or plastic contamination from the cap. High-alcohol ales, however, which continue to ferment in their corked bottles, should be stored on their sides.

The familiar Bass symbol, a red triangle, was registered in 1876 and is the world's oldest trademark.

Pennsylvania has had more breweries in its history than any other state. In 1910 alone, 119 of the state's towns had at least one licensed beer maker.

Beer-advertising matchbook covers have become sought-after collectibles on Internet auction sites. A 1916 matchbook promoting Brehm's Brewery in Baltimore sold for $43, while a 1930s cover promoting Eastside Beer from Los Angeles went for $36.

Beer and video games have a long association. Tapper, originally a 1983 arcade game and now a computer one, tests players' skills by challenging them to coordinate the movements of beers, a bartender, empty mugs, and patrons.

Nine people were killed and two houses destroyed on October 17, 1814, when a brewery tank containing 3,500 barrels of beer ruptured and created a giant wave.

According to a diary entry from a passenger on the *Mayflower*, the pilgrims made their landing at Plymouth Rock rather than continuing to their destination in Virginia due to a lack of beer.

The first canned beer was created on January 24, 1935. It was called Kruger Cream Ale and was sold by the Kruger Brewing Company of Richmond, Virginia.

The world's oldest known recipe is for beer.

In the United States, a barrel contains 31 gallons of beer.

Americans spend approximately $25 billion each year on beer.

In 1788, ale was proclaimed "the proper drink for Americans" at a parade in New York City.

George Washington had his own brewery on the grounds of Mount Vernon.

After consuming a bucket or two of vibrant brew they called *aul*, or ale, the Vikings would head fearlessly into battle, often without armor or even shirts. In fact, "berserk" means "bare shirt" in Norse, and eventually took on the meaning of their wild battles.

Twelve ounces of a typical American pale lager actually has fewer calories than the same serving of 2 percent milk or apple juice.

Vassar College was established and funded by a brewer.

Beer is believed to have been a staple before bread. In ancient Egypt, "bread and beer" was a common greeting. Early Egyptian writings urged mothers to send their children to school with plenty of bread and beer for their lunch.

Every year, Bavarians and their guests drink 1.2 million gallons of beer during Oktoberfest. The first Oktoberfest was in 1810 and celebrated the marriage of King Ludwig I of Bavaria. Despite the month implied by its name, the 16-day Oktoberfest actually begins in mid-September and ends on the first Sunday in October.

Early recipes for beer included such ingredients as poppy seeds, mushrooms, aromatics, honey, sugar, bay leaves, butter, and breadcrumbs.

British men are twice as likely to know the price of beer as their partner's bra size. A poll by *Prima* magazine found that 77 percent of males knew how much their beer cost, but only 38 percent knew the correct size of their partner's bra.

A labeorphilist is a collector of beer bottles.

One brand of Chinese beer reportedly includes in its recipe "ground-up dog parts."

In Bangladesh, $5 will buy a beer . . . or a first-class train ticket for a cross-country trip.

❧ BREW BELIEFS

If a young Tiriki man offers beer to a woman and she spits some of it into his mouth, they are engaged to be married.

Among the Bagonda people of Uganda, the widows of a recently deceased king have the distinctive honor of drinking the beer in which his entrails have been cleaned.

The Chagga people of Tanzania believe that a liar will be poisoned if he or she consumes beer mixed with the blood of a recently sacrificed goat.

Beer is mixed with saliva and blood for a drink that is shared when two men of the Chagga tribe become blood brothers.

Some people in Malaysia wash their babies in beer to protect them from diseases.

In ancient Babylon, women brewers also assumed the role of temple priestesses. The Goddess Siris was the patron of beer.

BOTTOMS UP

Distilled spirits (whiskey, brandy, rum, tequila, gin, etc.) contain no carbohydrates, no fats of any kind, and no cholesterol.

"White lightning" is a name for illegally distilled spirits. All spirits are clear or "white" until aged in charred oak barrels.

It is estimated that the United States government takes in 14 times more in taxes on distilled spirits than producers of the products earn making them. That does not include what states and localities additionally take in taxes on the same products.

"Whiskey" is the international aviation word used to represent the letter W. Whiskey and whisky both refer to alcohol distilled from grain. Whiskey is the usual American spelling, especially for beverages distilled in the United States and Ireland. Whisky is the spelling for Canadian and Scotch distilled beverages.

Scotch whisky's distinctive smoky flavor comes from drying malted barley over peat fires.

Rye was the first distinctly American whiskey. It is distilled from a combination of corn, barley malt, and at least 51 percent rye.

The highest price ever paid for distilled spirits at auction was $79,552 for a 50-year-old bottle of Glenfiddich whisky in 1992.

Bourbon is the official spirit of the United States, by act of Congress. Bourbon takes its name from Bourbon County in Kentucky, where it was first produced in 1789 by a Baptist minister, although Bourbon County no longer produces bourbon.

Gin is spirit alcohol flavored from juniper berries. First made by the Dutch, it was called *junever*, the Dutch word for juniper. The French called it *genievre*, which the English changed to *geneva* and then modified to gin.

Gin is a mild diuretic, which helps the body get rid of excessive fluid. Thus it can reduce problems such as menstrual bloating. In the nineteenth century, people believed that gin could cure stomach problems. Gin and tonic is still thought to help relieve cramps.

Sloe gin is not gin at all but a liqueur made with sloe berries (blackthorn bush berries).

Vodka ("little water") is the Russian name for grain spirits without flavor added.

The most popular gift in Eastern Europe is a bottle of vodka.

Vodka has been the largest-selling distilled spirit in the United States for over 25 years, and one of every four alcohol drinks consumed in the world is vodka or vodka-based.

"Brandy" is from the Dutch *brandewijn*, meaning burned (or distilled) wine.

In the seventeenth century, thermometers were filled with brandy instead of mercury.

In the nineteenth century, rum was considered excellent for cleaning hair and keeping it healthy. Brandy was believed to strengthen hair roots.

Rum was issued daily to every sailor in the British navy from 1651 until 1970.

L'Esprit de Courvoisier, a cognac made from brandies distilled between 1802 and 1931, sells for around $150 a shot.

The letters VVSOP on a cognac bottle stand for Very Very Superior Old Pale.

The words "cordial" and "liqueur" are synonymous and refer to liquors made of sweetened spirits flavored with fruits, flowers, roots, or other organic materials.

The Asian cordial koumiss is made of fermented cow's milk.

Kinpaku-iri sake contains flakes of real gold. While this adds a touch of extravagance, it doesn't affect the flavor at all.

Shochu, a beverage distilled from barley, was the favorite beverage of the world's longest-living man, Shigechiyo Izumi of Japan, who reportedly lived for 120 years and 237 days.

Colonial New Englanders often put barrels of hard cider outdoors in cold weather, then removed the ice to increase the alcohol content of the remaining beverage.

Mead is a beverage made of a fermented honey and water mixture.

Tequila is made from the root of the blue agave cactus.

There is no worm in tequila. It's in mezcal, a spirit beverage distilled from a different plant. And it's not actually a worm, but a moth caterpillar (*Hipopta agavis*). When the worm is included, the drink is known as *con gusano*, or "with worm."

COCKTALES

Writer H. L. Mencken determined that 17,864,392,788 different cocktails could be made from the ingredients in a well-stocked bar.

Although the origins of the martini are obscure, it likely actually began as a sweet drink.

Adding a miniature onion to a martini turns it into a Gibson.

A tequini is a martini made with tequila instead of dry gin.

In a martini competition in Chicago, the winner was a martini made with an anchovy-stuffed olive that was served in a glass that had been rinsed with Cointreau liqueur.

A mixed drink containing a carbonated beverage is absorbed into the body more quickly than straight shots are.

A popular drink during the Middle Ages to soothe those

who were sick and heal them was called a caudle. It was an alcohol drink containing eggs, bread, sugar, and spices.

The Manhattan cocktail (whiskey and sweet vermouth) was invented by Winston Churchill's mother.

Mai Tai means "out of this world" in Tahitian.

"Cocktails for Hitler" weren't drinks at all. During World War II, distillers shifted all production to industrial alcohol for the war effort. Hence, they were making "cocktails for Hitler."

The mint julep was once a very popular everyday drink, the Coca-Cola of its time.

WINE AND DINE

The wine district of the Napa Valley has replaced Disneyland as California's number one tourist destination, with 5.5 million visitors per year.

The California grape and wine industries were largely started by Count Agoston Haraszthy de Moksa, who planted Tokay, Zinfandel, and Shiraz varieties from his native Hungary in Buena Vista in 1857.

The largest cork tree in the world is in Portugal. It averages over one ton of raw cork per harvest, enough to cork 100,000 bottles.

The soil of one famous vineyard in France is considered so precious that vineyard workers are required to scrape it from their shoes before they leave for home each night.

In Utah, it is illegal to swallow wine served at tastings.

"Fat Bastard Chardonnay" is a French wine label.

British wine is different from English wine. British wine is made from imported grapes; English wine is not.

The vintage date on a bottle of wine indicates the year the grapes were picked, not the year of bottling.

Foot-treading of grapes is still used in producing a small quantity of the best port wines.

Vintage port can take 40 years to reach maturity.

A *trokenbeerenauslese* is a type of German wine made from vine-dried grapes that are so rare, it can take a skilled picker a day to gather enough for just one bottle.

Christopher Columbus introduced sherry to the New World.

During the winter months, the Romans of the Mosel wine region would drink their wine hot, like a tea.

No government health warning is permitted on wine imported into any country in the European Union.

One of every five glasses of wine consumed in the world is sake.

"Muscatel" means "wine with flies in it" in Italian.

Poor soil tends to produce better wines.

White wine is usually produced from red grapes.

Most wines do not improve with age.

As late as the mid-seventeenth century, French wine-makers did not use corks. Instead, they used oil-soaked rags stuffed into the necks of bottles.

Wine has about the same number of calories as an equal amount of grape juice.

White wine gets darker as it ages while red wine gets lighter.

The corkscrew was invented in 1860.

Most European grapevines are planted on American grape rootstock.

French chemist Louis Pasteur, best known for creating

the pasteurization process and the first rabies vaccine, owned a vineyard in the Jura wine region that is still producing wine today.

The indentation at the bottom of some wine bottles is called a kick or a punt. The purpose of the indentation is not for the wine waiter to put his fingers, but to strengthen the structure of the bottle.

During World War II, a group of alpine soldiers who were stranded in mountain snows survived for an entire month on one cask of sherry.

It takes an average number of 600 grapes to make a bottle of wine.

An award-winning adaptation of *Little Red Riding Hood* was withdrawn from a recommended reading list by the school board in Culver City, California, simply because the heroine had included a bottle of wine in the basket she brought to her grandmother.

Vermouth is a white appetizer wine flavored with up to 40 to 50 different berries, herbs, roots, seeds, and flowers, and takes about a year to make.

The Romans drank a wine containing seawater, pitch, rosin, and turpentine.

The Lombardy wine region of Franciacorta produces a style of sparkling wine that is more bubbly than frizzante but has less carbon dioxide than most sparkling wines.

The entire production of kosher wine, including cultivation of the grapes, must be performed by Sabbath-observant Jews, and it remains kosher only if opened and poured by an orthodox Jew.

A BIT OF THE BUBBLY

The shallow champagne glass originated with Marie Antoinette. It was first formed from wax molds made of her breasts.

Champagne is bottled in eight sizes: bottle, magnum (2 bottles), jeroboam (4 bottles), rehoboam (6 bottles), Methuselah (8 bottles), Salamanca (12 bottles), Balthazar (16 bottles), and Nebuchadnezzar (20 bottles).

A raisin dropped in a glass of fresh champagne will bounce up and down continually from the bottom of the glass to the top.

The longest recorded champagne cork flight was 177 feet and 9 inches, 4 feet from level ground, at Woodbury Vineyards in New York State.

There are an estimated 49 million bubbles in a bottle of champagne. Bubbles were seen by early winemakers as a highly undesirable defect to be prevented.

The pressure in a bottle of champagne is about 90 pounds per square inch. That's about three times the pressure in car tires.

A NATIONAL PASTIME

The United States has the highest minimum drinking age in the entire world.

The *Mayflower* ordinarily transported alcohol between Spain and England.

More than half of the hospitals in the largest 65 metropolitan areas in the United States have reported that they offer an alcohol beverage service to their patients.

Of Texas's 254 counties, 79 are still completely dry seven decades after the repeal of Prohibition. Many of the remaining counties are "moist," or partially dry. The county in Texas with the highest DWI arrests among young drivers is dry.

In 1926, Montana became the first state to repeal its enforcement of Prohibition.

Franklin D. Roosevelt was elected president in 1932 on a pledge to end national Prohibition.

Rhode Island never ratified the Eighteenth Amendment establishing Prohibition.

There are 83 dry towns and villages in Alaska.

The longest bar in the world is 684 feet long and is located at the New Bulldog in Rock Island, Illinois.

The space in the New York City building that once housed the National Temperance Society is now a bar.

The founder of MADD (Mothers Against Drunk Driving) resigned after it became increasingly anti-alcohol rather than simply anti–drunk driving.

The Marines' first recruiting station was in a bar.

First Lady Martha Washington enjoyed daily toddies.

Tom Arnold, Sandra Bullock, Chevy Chase, Bill Cosby, Kris Kristofferson, and Bruce Willis are all former bartenders.

President Lincoln, when informed that General Grant drank whiskey while leading his troops, reportedly replied, "Find out the name of the brand so I can give it to my other generals." He also once stated, "It has long been recognized that the problems with alcohol relate not to the use of a bad thing, but to the abuse of a good thing."

The bill for a celebration party for the 55 drafters of the U.S. Constitution was for 54 bottles of Madeira, 60 bottles of claret, 8 bottles of whiskey, 22 bottles of port, 8 bottles of hard cider, 12 beers, and 7 bowls of alcohol punch large enough that "ducks could swim in them."

The national anthem, "The Star-Spangled Banner," was written to the tune of a British drinking song.

Liquor stores in the United States are called "package stores" and sell "package goods" because of laws requiring that alcohol containers be concealed in public by being placed in paper bags or "packages." The word "liquor" is prohibited on storefronts in some states.

The term "brand name" originated among American distillers, who branded their names and emblems on their kegs before shipment.

The region of the United States that consumes the least alcohol (commonly known as the "Bible belt") is also known by many doctors as Stroke Alley.

In West Virginia, bars can advertise alcohol beverage prices, but not brand names.

President Thomas Jefferson was the nation's first wine expert.

In Utah it's illegal to advertise drink prices and alcohol brands, to show a "drinking scene," to promote happy hour, to advertise free food, or for restaurants to furnish alcohol beverage lists unless a customer specifically requests one.

A Florida man who was arrested for drunk driving was found innocent of the charge when he proved before a jury that the alcohol officers had smelled on his breath was from the mixture of rubbing alcohol and gasoline that he had just used in his performance as a professional fire-breather.

Men in the United States who drink alcohol receive about 7 percent higher wages than do abstainers, according to data from the National Household Survey on Drug Abuse. Women who drink receive about 3.5 percent higher wages than do abstainers.

William Sokolin paid $519,750 for a bottle of 1787 vintage wine that supposedly had been owned by President Thomas Jefferson, then later accidentally knocked it over, breaking it and spilling the precious contents on the floor.

Of all the countries who had armies stationed in Bosnia, only the United States forbade its soldiers from consuming alcohol.

In Pennsylvania, the tax on wine and spirits is called the Johnstown Flood tax because it was imposed in 1936 to raise funds to help the city recover from a devastating flood. The city was quickly rebuilt, but the tax continues, costing state taxpayers over $160 million each year.

Johnny Appleseed probably distributed apple seeds across the American frontier so that people could make fermented apple juice (hard cider) rather than eat apples.

SPIRITS IN SOCIETY

The top 10 alcohol-consuming countries are Portugal, Luxembourg, France, Hungary, Spain, Czech Republic, Denmark, Germany, Austria, and Switzerland.

In Europe and North America, lower-status people tend to prefer beer whereas upper-status people tend to prefer wine and distilled spirits. In Latin America and Africa, lower-class people tend to drink home-brew, middle-class people bottled beer, and upper-class people distilled spirits.

Drinking chocolate mixed with beverage alcohol was fashionable at European social events in the seventeenth century.

Alcohol is considered the only proper payment for teachers among the Lepcha people of Tibet.

The Uape Indians of the Upper Amazon in Brazil mix the ashes of their cremated dead with *casiri*, the local alcohol beverage. The deceased's family then drink the beverage with great reverence and fond memories.

The Aztecs of Mexico used a "rabbit scale" to describe degrees of intoxication. It ranged from very mild intoxication (a few rabbits) to heavy drunkenness (400 rabbits).

Vikings used the skulls of their enemies as drinking vessels.

Chicha, an alcohol beverage that has been made for thousands of years in Central and South America, begins with people chewing grain and spitting into a vat. An enzyme in the saliva changes starch in the grain to sugar, which then ferments.

McDonald's restaurants in some European countries serve alcohol because otherwise parents would be less willing to take their children to them.

In 2003, thousands of waxwing birds in Sweden became intoxicated by gorging on fermenting rowanberries. About 50 lost their lives by flying into nearby windows.

There is one bar in Paris that serves only bottled and canned water.

In English pubs, ale is ordered by pints and quarts. In old England when customers got unruly, the bartender would yell at them to mind their own pints and quarts and settle down. This is where we get the phrase "Mind your Ps and Qs."

Many years ago in England, pub-goers had a whistle baked into the rim or handle of their ceramic cups. When they needed a refill, they used the whistle to get some service, which inspired the phrase "Wet your whistle."

In Queensland, Australia, it is still constitutional law that all pubs must have a railing outside for patrons to tie up their horses.

Adolf Hitler was one of the world's best-known teetotalers, while his counterpart Sir Winston Churchill was one of the world's best-known heavy drinkers.

In Bavaria, beer isn't considered an alcoholic drink, but rather a staple food.

The word "toast," meaning a wish of good health, started in ancient Rome, where a piece of toasted bread was dropped into wine.

Do you like *isyammitilka* or *ksikonewiw*? Those are the words for alcohol beverages among the Alabama and the Maliseet-Passamaquoddy tribes of American Indians.

In Malaysia, drunk drivers are jailed and so are their spouses.

In some countries the penalty for driving while intoxicated can be death.

In Uruguay, intoxication is a legal excuse for having an accident while driving.

Among the Abipone people of Paraguay, individuals

who abstain from alcohol are thought to be "cowardly, degenerate, and stupid."

Outfitting his ship to sail around the world in 1519, Magellan spent more on sherry than on weapons.

Frederick the Great of Prussia tried to ban the consumption of coffee and demanded that the populace drink alcohol instead.

The Soviet Bolsheviks imposed national prohibition following the Russian revolution.

During the reign of William III, a garden fountain was once used as a giant punch bowl. The punch recipe included 560 gallons of brandy, 1,200 pounds of sugar, 25,000 lemons, 20 gallons of lime juice, and 5 pounds of nutmeg. The bartender rowed around in a small boat, filling up guests' punch cups.

I Love Lucy star Desi Arnaz's grandfather was one of the founders of the largest rum distillery in the world.

MOVIE MAGIC

ON A ROLE

Cary Grant was offered the role of James Bond and refused it before the producers offered it to Sean Connery.

Leonard Nimoy owned a pet store in the 1960s before playing Mr. Spock in *Star Trek*.

In the first *Terminator* film, Arnold Schwarzenegger had only 17 lines of dialogue.

David Niven's voice had to be dubbed in on *Curse of the Pink Panther* by Canadian impersonator Rich Little. Niven was so ill while filming that he could not speak. It was his last role and he died the year the film was released, in 1983.

In the 1944 movie *Arsenic and Old Lace*, the character of Jonathan, a murderer on the run from the police, has his face accidentally disguised by his alcoholic accomplice to look like actor Boris Karloff in his famous role as Frankenstein's monster. This was a reference to the fact that Karloff had played the role of Jonathan in the original stage production on which the movie was based.

Actress Taylor Fry, who played Lucy McClane, Bruce Willis's character's daughter in *Die Hard*, auditioned to reprise the role in the film's third sequel *Live Free or Die Hard*, but was rejected.

Julia Roberts and Daniel Day-Lewis were the original actors cast as the leads in *Shakespeare in Love*; the roles eventually went to Gwyneth Paltrow and Joseph Fiennes.

Actress Maggie Smith, then 38 years old, played a character more than forty years older than her actual age in the film *Travels with My Aunt*. She was nine years younger than the actor playing her nephew in the film.

The role of Dr. Peter Venkman in *Ghostbusters* was originally intended for John Belushi, but went to Bill Murray after Belushi's death. Some people involved in the making of the film have suggested that Murray never even read the script and improvised most of his lines.

Richard Gere has played roles that John Travolta turned down three times with great success, in the movies *An Officer and a Gentleman*, *American Gigolo*, and *Chicago*. Sean Connery was originally approached to play Hannibal Lector in *The Silence of the Lambs*, but declined. Anthony Hopkins, who only appears in the film for 16 minutes, won an Oscar for the part—the shortest lead role to ever win an Oscar.

REEL LIFE

In 2007 a court in Naples, Italy, summoned Donald Duck, along with his girlfriend Daisy, Mickey Mouse, and Tweety Bird, to appear as damaged parties in the criminal trial of a Chinese man accused of counterfeiting products of Disney and Warner Bros. Lawyers think it was a clerical error.

Marilyn Monroe's ex-husband Joe DiMaggio had fresh roses delivered to her crypt three times a week for 20 years after her death.

The real names of Dean Martin and Jerry Lewis were Dino Paul Croccetti and Jerome Levitch.

The inscription on Rodney Dangerfield's tombstone reads: There goes the neighborhood.

The most copied noses in Hollywood are those of Heather Locklear, Nicole Kidman, and Catherine Zeta-Jones.

The real names of Fred Astaire and Ginger Rogers were Frederic Austerlitz Jr. and Virginia Katherine McMath.

Film star Audrey Hepburn was fluent in English, French, Dutch, Flemish, Spanish, and Italian, and was a member of the Dutch Resistance in World War II at age 15.

Before he became a film actor, Humphrey Bogart, as the house player for an arcade, charged 50 cents a game to people who wanted to play chess.

Before they became successful in show business, Charles Bronson and Jack Palance both labored as coal miners, as did Ava Gardner's father.

David Manning was the name of a fictitious film critic created by a Sony employee to provide glowing reviews for the company's upcoming movies in 2000. After the deception was discovered, Sony made an out-of-court settlement in 2005 promising to refund $5 to anyone who saw the affected movies during their theatrical runs: *Hollow Man*, *The Animal*, *The Patriot*, *A Knight's Tale*, and *Vertical Limit*.

A new biography of Laurence Olivier suggests that he was recruited during World War II to be an undercover agent for the British government in America on the suggestion of Winston Churchill.

Iconic actresses and sisters Joan Fontaine and Olivia de Havilland have reportedly not spoken since 1975 due to a family feud.

Actor Clint Howard, brother of film director Ron Howard, is known to be an avid fan of the online role-playing game *World of Warcraft*, where he plays a Level 70 Orc Hunter named Extas.

FILM FLUBS

The man who opened the world's first movie theater in Paris said, "The cinema is an invention without any commercial future."

There were 207 spottable mistakes in *Star Wars*, the most found so far in any movie. Second highest was *Harry Potter and the Chamber of Secrets* with 203 mistakes, and third was *Pirates of the Caribbean: The Curse of the Black Pearl* with 201.

In the movie *Rear Window*, Grace Kelly is in a scene arguing with James Stewart, who is sitting in a wheelchair with a cast on his leg. The cast switches from his left leg to his right during the scene.

In the movie *The Breakfast Club*, Molly Ringwald's character can be seen putting away her tube of lipstick twice after applying it in a memorable fashion by holding the tube in place with her cleavage.

In *Camelot*, when Richard Harris as King Arthur makes a speech praising his subjects and realm, he has a modern Band-Aid on his neck.

The 1948 comedy *June Bride*, which filmed two versions of a line that referenced the candidates to the 1948 presidency, opened in theaters with the wrong future president named. Thomas Dewey seemed a sure win, so the Dewey line was retained in the original release. When Harry Truman unexpectedly won the election, a revised reel was sent to theaters. Star Bette Davis, a Truman supporter, had her costar, Dewey supporter Robert Montgomery, send Dewey a gloating telegram.

Al Capone is shown living in a sumptuous Chicago mansion in the film *The St. Valentine's Day Massacre*. In fact, he lived in a small house in a working-class district of the city.

> *The Bridge on the River Kwai* won seven Oscars, but star Alec Guinness's name was misspelled in the credits as Alec Guiness.

In the movie *Gladiator*, when one of the chariots flips over in the Coliseum, a gas tank can be seen on its under-carriage.

> Although *Mr. and Mrs. Smith* is supposed to take place around New York City, in a chase scene a street sign can clearly be seen indicating they are in Los Angeles.

In *Indiana Jones and the Last Crusade*, when Indiana is masquerading as a Scot to gain access to a Nazi strong-hold, the butler audibly says, "If you are a Scottish lord, then I am Mickey Mouse," but the movements of his mouth indicate that he is actually saying ". . . then I am Jesse Owens," which was the original line and was changed in post-production because the filmmakers felt that audiences wouldn't get the joke.

> In *The Usual Suspects*, when a character flings a lit cigarette at actor Stephen Baldwin and hits him in the face, Baldwin's reaction is real as the cigarette was supposed to hit him in the chest.

TINSELTOWN MENAGERIE

Only three dogs have a star in the Hollywood Walk of Fame: Strongheart, Rin Tin Tin, and Lassie.

Pete the Pup, a pit bull mix that appeared in the *Our Gang* shorts, had a fresh circle drawn around his right eye before every shoot.

The highest-paid animal actors are bears, which can earn $20,000 a day.

The 1967 film *Doctor Dolittle* featured the last performance of chimpanzee actor Cheeta, who appeared in many of the *Tarzan* films of the 1930s and 1940s. Now retired, Cheeta celebrated his seventy-fifth birthday on April 9, 2007, and is listed in the Guinness Book of World Records as the world's oldest (non-human) primate.

CINEMA SNIPPETS

The longest film title was *Night of the Day of the Dawn of the Son of the Bride of the Return of the Revenge of the Terror of the Attack of the Evil, Mutant, Alien, Flesh-Eating, Hellbound Zombified Living Dead Part 2: In Shocking 2-D* in 1991.

It took four months to synchronize the three-minute scene between live actors and animated skeletons in *Jason and the Argonauts*.

The DVD release of the 1999 Tim Allen comedy *Galaxy Quest* includes an alternate audio track in which dialogue from the film is overdubbed in the aliens' "Thermian" language.

The 1999 movie *South Park: Bigger Longer and Uncut* has the dubious distinction of containing the most swear words in any film, 399, and the most offensive gestures, 128.

Flutist Masakazu Yoshizawa was hired by composer John Williams to play the *shakuhachi*, a Japanese bamboo flute similar to a recorder, for the *Jurassic Park* soundtrack because he thought the instrument sounded like a dinosaur's cry.

Legend has it that when Alfred Hitchcock bought the film rights for the novel on which *Psycho* is based, he bought as many copies of the book as he could find to try to keep audiences from discovering the ending.

Both Bruce Willis and his stunt double were injured in separate accidents during the filming of 2007's *Live Free or Die Hard*.

The famous Omaha Beach landing sequence in *Saving Private Ryan* was actually filmed in Ireland. The 24-minute long scene cost $11 million and utilized about a thousand extras, including members of the IRA and actual amputees who portrayed U.S. soldiers maimed during the attack.

The music budget for the film *Almost Famous*, which includes more than 50 songs, was reported to be about $3.5 million, compared to less than $1.5 million on average for most films.

As of December 2007, the Disney film *Toy Story 2* is the only film to have more than 100 positive reviews and no negative ones on the popular film review website www.rottentomatoes.com.

The 12 jurors in the movie *12 Angry Men* are not called by their names during any of the deliberations; the only jurors whose names are discovered at the end of the movie are the last names of Joseph Sweeney and Henry Fonda's characters—McArdle and Davis.

Madonna earned the Guinness World Record for most costume changes in a film for her role in *Evita*, beating Elizabeth Taylor's record for *Cleopatra*. Madonna's 85 costume changes included 39 hats, 45 pairs of shoes, and 56 pairs of earrings.

Babe, a family film about a talking pig, was initially banned in Malaysia due to its title and the fact that its subject matter was not halal.

The tag line for the 1963 comedy *Under the Yum Yum Tree*, starring Jack Lemmon as a lascivious landlord, was "A delicious sexual frolic for all Jack Lemmon fans!"

Tom Jones is the only film in history to have three cast members nominated for the Academy Award for Best Supporting Actress—none of them won, though the film did win Best Picture.

The screenwriter for the film *Sister Act* requested that his name not appear on the final draft of the film since it had gone through many rewrites by other people. He initially suggested the writer's credit be changed to "screenplay by Goofy," but when that was rejected he came up with the pseudonym Joseph Howard.

The film *Splash* is often credited with popularizing the name "Madison" for girls, as that is the name the mermaid played by Darryl Hannah chooses for herself after seeing it on a street sign on Madison Avenue in New York City.

The band Aerosmith was stumped trying to find lyrics for what would become their hit song "Walk This Way" until they took a break and went to a screening of the movie *Young Frankenstein*, where they were inspired by the famous "walk this way" gag.

Among the actors cut out of the final version of *The Thin Red Line* during the editing process were Billy Bob Thornton, Martin Sheen, Gary Oldman, Jason Patric, Bill Pullman, Lukas Haas, Viggo Mortensen, and Mickey Rourke. John Travolta and George Clooney's roles were significantly reduced as well.

The title of the film *The Usual Suspects* refers to a line in *Casablanca*.

All the characters in the movie *His Girl Friday* were originally supposed to be male, but the director liked the way his secretary read the male reporter's lines and rewrote the script to make the character female and the ex-wife of Cary Grant's character.

Dalton Trumbo, one of the writers of the classic *Roman Holiday*, was not credited on the film until its DVD release in 2003 as he was on the Hollywood blacklist when the film came out in 1953.

Before the MPAA film-rating system currently in use was established, films made for American audiences had to adhere to the U.S. Motion Picture Production Code. This code stated that, among other things, ridicule of religion, interracial relationships, and depictions of crimes (such as smuggling or arson) were forbidden, along with "revenge in modern times." This sometimes necessitated changes when films were adapted from novels; for instance, in the novel *Rebecca*, the husband shoots his wife, while in the film he only *thinks* about killing her, whereupon she conveniently falls and is fatally injured.

Although *A Christmas Story* is set in Indiana, the house where main character Ralphie lived is on Cleveland's West Side. It has been restored, reconfigured on the interior to match the soundstage layouts from the movie, and is open to the public.

In the movie *Rosemary's Baby*, when Mia Farrow's character calls another character on the phone, her real-life good friend, actor Tony Curtis, played the voice on the other line, unknown to her; thus her confusion on screen is real as she tries to place the familiar voice.

The director of the film *Trainspotting* has stated that he would like to make a sequel to the film but is waiting until the original actors have aged enough to show a passage of time. He jokingly commented that due to the natural vanity of actors, it might be a long wait.

Although the children's movie *Finding Nemo* portrays the practice of catching fish for pets in a negative light, the movie's popularity caused a surge in demand for pet clownfish (the species of the title character).

After the success of the movie *Braveheart*, a statue of Mel Gibson as William Wallace was placed outside the Wallace Monument in Scotland. This upset locals so much that someone vandalized the face of the statue, causing it to be locked in a cage at night for protection—ironically negating the word "freedom," which is carved on the plinth.

A "dollar baby" is a term used by author Stephen King to describe the group of aspiring filmmakers or theater producers to whom he has granted permission to create a non-commercial adaptation of one of his short stories for one dollar. Currently about 50 such projects are known to have been made, including a short by director Frank Darabont, who went on to direct three more King stories and novels as feature films: *The Shawshank Redemption*, *The Green Mile*, and *The Mist*.

In 1994 *Schindler's List* became the first Oscar-winning movie to also be nominated for an MTV Movie Award for Best Movie. It lost to *Menace 2 Society*, which was not nominated for any Oscars. The same year, Tom Hanks became the only Oscar winner for Best Actor to also win the Best Male Performance category at the MTV Awards, for his role in *Philadelphia*.

The 2004 film *The Motorcycle Diaries*, while well-reviewed, could not be nominated for a Best Foreign Language Film Oscar because it had no specific country of origin as the cast, crew, director, and shooting locations were all affiliated with different nations; therefore, no country would claim it as their official entry.

The Lord of the Rings: The Return of the King was the first-ever fantasy film to win the Oscar for Best Picture. It won all eleven categories it was nominated in, tying the records of *Titanic* and *Ben-Hur*.

As of 2007 only five horror films have been nominated for an Academy Award for Best Picture: *The Exorcist*, *Jaws*, *A Clockwork Orange*, *The Silence of the Lambs*, and *The Sixth Sense*. *The Silence of the Lambs* was the only winner.

The film *Exit to Eden* was briefly banned in Saskatchewan upon its release, which puzzled many people as it was the only place to ban the film.

Although the English title of the 2006 Spanish film *El Laberinto del Fauno* is *Pan's Labyrinth*, the director has stated that the faun who appears in the film is not meant to be the Greek god Pan.

M. Night Shyamalan has said that he got the idea for the plot of *The Sixth Sense* from an episode of the Nickelodeon TV series *Are You Afraid of the Dark?*

Some residents of Odessa, Texas, claim that the football team featured in the 1999 film *Varsity Blues* is based on their high school team the Permian Panthers. Whether or not this is true, the Panthers were the basis for the book, movie, and TV series *Friday Night Lights*.

The scene in the movie *Entrapment* where Catherine Zeta-Jones slinks her body through a maze of lasers was choreographed by the same man who choreographed the wand battles in *Harry Potter and the Order of the Phoenix*.

The second film in the Austin Powers series, *Austin Powers: The Spy Who Shagged Me*, grossed more money in its opening weekend than the entire box-office take of the first film.

Disney's 1999 animated film *Tarzan* had a budget of $150 million, making it currently the most expensive Disney animated film ever made.

The character of Elektra King from *The World Is Not Enough* is the only woman to be considered the main villain in a James Bond movie, as opposed to just an accomplice.

The line "You can't handle the truth!" from *A Few Good Men* was voted the twenty-ninth greatest American movie quote of all time by the American Film Institute.

The DVD packaging for *Teenage Mutant Ninja Turtles III* refers to the main characters as "American's favorite amphibians," though turtles are actually reptiles.

In the 1993 *Demolition Man* one of the names on the Los Angeles cryoprison's prisoners list in 2032 is Scott Peterson—coincidentally that is the name of the man convicted in 2005 of murdering his wife, Laci, and their unborn child in a high-profile case.

For the movie *The Interpreter*, which is about political unrest in the fictitious African Republic of Matobo, the filmmakers hired the director of the Centre for African Language Learning in England to invent a language called Ku, which is actually a cross between the Swahili and Shona languages.

A FRESH TAKE

Success is a great deodorant. It takes away all your past smells.

Elizabeth Taylor

The duration of a film should not exceed the capacity of the human bladder.

Alfred Hitchcock

At Last

Telesphobia: The fear of being last.